THE H Com

A Practical Approach to a Meaningful Life

His Holiness the XIV Dalai Lama

LOTUS PRESS
Twin Lakes, WI

Foundation for
Universal Responsibility
of His Holiness
the Dalai Lama

FULL CIRCLE

First published in India in 2001 by Full Circle Publishing under arrangement and by association with the Foundation for Universal Responsibility.

First U.S. edition November 2002 by Lotus Press. Published by agreement with the Foundation of Universal Responsibility.

Contact Lotus Press, P.O. Box 325, Twin Lakes, Wisconsin 53181. Web: www.lotuspress.com   Email: lotuspress@lotuspress.com (800) 824-6396

Library of Congress Cataloging-in-Publication Data
HH Dalai Lama
The Heart of Compassion, A Practical Approach to a Meaningful Life
ISBN: 0-940985-36-5 (Paperbound)
ISBN: 0-940985-38-1 (Hardbound)
1. Subject   I. Title
Library of Congress Control Number: 2002107661 (Paperbound)
Library of Congress Control Number: 2002111771 (Hardbound))

Printed in the United States of America

Contents

Introduction

The Foundation for Universal Responsibility is honoured and delighted to present *The Heart of Compassion: A Practical Approach to a Meaningful Life*. We hope it will serve as an introduction to the vision, both Buddhist and secular, of a revered contemporary statesman and spiritual master. Though he embodies the aspirations of a free Tibet and the survival of its unique heritage, his message of universal responsibility, of compassion, altruism and peace have made him a spokesman for our troubled times. This collection, the first in a series of readers, includes the Dalai Lama's thoughts and teachings on secular techniques and practices of mind training, introductory Buddhism and a range of human concerns.

To more than six million of his people, the Dalai Lama is known as Yeshi Norbu, the precious Wish-Fulfilling Gem — the reincarnation of the Buddha aspect of compassion, Avalokiteshwara. To others, he is known by his Mongol title — The Dalai Lama or Ocean of Wisdom. To the more initiated, he is quite simply, His Holiness. He describes himself as Tenzin Gyatso, a simple Buddhist monk.

Born of peasant parents on July 6th 1935, he was recognised as the reincarnation of his predecessor — the great XIII Dalai Lama, the spiritual and temporal ruler of Tibet. He was educated in the rigorous tradition of Tibetan Buddhist monkhood from the age of six. He completed his Geshe Lharampa Degree (Doctor of Philosophy) with honours when he was twenty-five. At sixteen, he was obliged to assume political authority and power, at the urgings of his people, as the expanding Chinese empire threatened to overwhelm Tibet. In 1959, after years of fruitless attempts at negotiations with China, on a night of popular uprising against the Chinese in the capital city of Lhasa, the Dalai Lama was forced to flee Tibet. More than a million Tibetans died; of the more than ten thousand monasteries forty-five survived; and more than 150,000 have followed him into exile in India.

For more than four decades, the Dalai Lama has been in exile, as Chinese oppression in Tibet has continued, as has the systematic decimation of its culture and heritage. He has remained a transient on a refugee's passport, dependent on the generosity of foreigners. While India has been hospitable to this heir of the Buddhist tradition that began in the country more than 2500 years ago, it has often seemed indifferent to the political agenda of a free Tibet. The Dalai Lama has often described the relationship of Tibet with India as that of a student with its Guru. While the Dalai Lama is increasingly welcomed at the religious and political capitals of the world, Beijing continues to roar at the merest mention of his name. The Dalai Lama's humble sermons, spoken softly, are now proclaimed around a world that will perhaps yet find the will to act with the kind of courage that this simple monk himself embodies. Appeasement of the Chinese has prompted most political leaders to acknowledge him as a great religious figure divorced from the repression of his people. In 1989, in awarding the Nobel Peace Prize to the Dalai Lama, the Nobel Committee paid the public tribute that the billions outside China endorse:

The Norwegian Nobel Committee has decided to award the 1989 Nobel Peace Prize to the XIV Dalai Lama, Tenzin Gyatso, the religious and political leader of the Tibetan people. The committee wants to emphasise that the Dalai Lama in his struggle for the liberation of Tibet has consistently opposed the use of violence. He has instead advocated peaceful solutions based upon tolerance and mutual respect in order to preserve the historical and cultural heritage of his people. The Dalai Lama has developed his philosophy of peace from a great reverence of all things living and upon the concept of universal responsibility embracing all mankind as well as nature. In the opinion of the committee the Dalai Lama has come forward with constructive and forward looking proposals for the solution of international conflicts, human rights issues and global environmental problems.

The core of the Buddhist path is the recognition that life is an endless round of suffering, disease, death and rebirth, a cycle caused by a desire bred of ignorance and of an innate misconception of reality. Liberation or enlightenment occurs through training and disciplining of the mind. In time, the mind itself is transcended. There is then an innate experience of the true nature of reality, the recognition that all matter exists only in the manner of an illusion and in ultimate voidness. Buddhism, from its earliest forms, included the finest moral philosophy, with a vast range of mind development and pioneering psychology. As it travelled the globe, it evolved into religion, advanced philosophy, mysticism, metaphysics and the triple Yogas of India: the paths of reason, devotion and action. It was not enough to be taught human ideals; Buddhism became a practical adventure. His Holiness the Dalai Lama embodies this quest.

Forced out of the relative isolation of Tibet, the Dalai Lama has carried the essential insights of the Buddhist heritage with lightness and ease on his gentle, ever smiling face. The experiential empiricism of Buddhism has reached out to a dialogue in tune with the empiricism and the techniques of modern scientific method; the cultivation of altruism and deep insights into the reality of interdependence has bred a profound secular commitment and led to a meaningful dialogue. The Dalai Lama reaches out to a world increasingly responsive to his personality, teachings and message. His political cause is inextricably interwoven with the spiritual. That the Tibet of the future must be free to cultivate and pursue its rich heritage is a burden on the conscience of all mankind, not just the Dalai Lama.

The Foundation would like to thank the Library of Tibetan Works and Archives, Paljor Publications, Potala Publications, Wisdom Publications and Snow Lion for permission to publish extracts from the writings of His Holiness the Dalai Lama. It extends its appreciation to Raji Ramanan and Amit Jayaram in helping with the re-editing of the text, selecting passages and putting together the bibliography, glossary and other material. We would like to acknowledge the support of Poonam and Shekhar Malhotra of Full Circle Publishing Pvt. Ltd. and their continuing commitment to make available the writing and teachings of the Dalai Lama, primarily in India, but also overseas, as an ongoing collaborative initiative with the Foundation.

Rajiv Mehrotra
Trustee and Secretary

CHAPTER 1

The Need to Practise the Dharma

• •

The Tibetan word 'chos' is known as dharma in Sanskrit, and it means 'to hold'. All objects of this world that have definable identities are known as dharmas. There is another meaning of dharma, and this is 'to hold back from impending disaster'. It is in this sense that dharma can mean religion; religion, that is to say, as opposed to secularism. Generally speaking, any noble activity of mind, body or speech denotes dharma or religion — which can save one or hold one back from disaster. One is considered to practise religion if one implements these activities.

All wandering beings desire happiness and do not want suffering — not only intelligent humans, but also the foolish and close-minded, even the tiniest worms and insects. All desire happiness and do not wish to experience even the slightest suffering. Therefore, both I and others must engage in those means which give rise to happiness and do not bring about suffering. We require an ability to implement practices that initiate the causes from which happiness arises, and eliminate those that give rise to suffering.

Whatever we may do, there is no more perfect and complete means of establishing the causes of benefit and happiness, and the elimination of suffering and harm, than practising the dharma.

Relying on the dharma, we will be able to generate happiness and eliminate suffering in this life, the next life, and many future lifetimes. In this lifetime, for instance, there is nothing superior to practising the dharma for producing happiness and eliminating suffering. For example, there is a great difference between one who has understood the dharma and one who has not — with reference to the degree of their mental and physical suffering, and their ability to cope with it.

If the importance of the dharma is not understood, and the benefits of the teachings are not integrated with the mind, when there is a strong feeling of sickness in the body, the mind cannot bear it ; both body and mind are oppressed by great suffering, and the agony of pain negates the experience of happiness. If the importance of the dharma is understood, when the body experiences sickness, by seeing it as the result of previously accumulated wrong-doing, as being of the nature of cyclic existence, and through taking responsibility for the action by accepting the sickness, mental suffering will not be experienced. Consequently, external physical pain may be overcome by the inner power of mind, through which suffering will be dispelled. Therefore, mind is the principal factor controlling the body, and the mind's feelings of happiness or pain are more powerful than those of the body.

Any major or minor sufferings experienced in this life are the faults of either not understanding the dharma or being aware of it, but not putting it into practice.

If we practise the teachings, we will be able to stem the flow of all these sufferings. One might ask how this is possible. All such sufferings occur solely because of pride, miserliness and jealousy, the three delusions of attachment, aversion and ignorance, and so on. These faults of the mind are pacified and dispelled mainly by the power of the dharma; and contentment, a sense of shame, consideration and conscientiousness are adopted. Then, body and mind enjoy nothing but peace, calm and happiness — and unbearable pains do not arise. If we wish for joy and happiness in this life, and do not seek suffering, it is important to not only understand the essential meaning of the dharma, but also to put it into practice.

To practise in such a way is to gain predominantly. The happiness of this life is inadequate because, however great it is, it lasts only until death. However long life may be, it will not last more than 100 years, and just so long will that happiness endure. Since the trail of future lives is long and hazardous, we need to give it some direction. We should therefore strive for the means of finding happiness in, and eliminating suffering from, the stream of future lives. That too can be done only in conformity with the dharma, never in accordance with other activities.

When it is explained that the goals of future lives must be accomplished, there are some who do not understand the dharma — or who know a little, but do not grasp the reasoning perfectly — who may think that the present mind depends simply on this body and that, since past and future lives cannot be seen directly, they do not exist. Such an opinion either maintains that if something exists it must be seen directly, or that the mind is produced in dependence on the four elements, and, therefore, concludes that previous lives do not exist. It is thought that, at the time of death, the body reverts to the four principal elements, while the mind vanishes like a rainbow in the sky — and that, therefore, future lives do not exist. Others, asserting that the mind is dependent on the body, consider that, as the ability to intoxicate is an attribute of alcohol, so the mind is the attribute of the body. Essentially, all these views assert that, in this life, it is not necessary for the mind, which is produced at the time of birth, to be generated from a corresponding mind, because it is born from inanimate elements.

Nevertheless, despite various assertions, past and future lives certainly exist, for the following reasons. Certain ways of thinking from last year and the year before that, and even from childhood, can be recollected now. This clearly establishes that there existed an awareness previous to the present continuity of awareness of an adult. Likewise, the first instant of consciousness of this life is not produced without cause; nor is it born from something permanent; nor is it produced from a solid, inanimate, incongruent substantial cause; therefore, it must surely be produced from a congruent substantial cause

It is also unreasonable to think that past or future lives do not exist because they are not seen directly, for it is unacceptable to assert the non-existence of something merely because we have not seen it ourselves. We can understand this, in our age of science and technology, from our experience of seeing and hearing of many new external and internal discoveries, of which our forefathers in past centuries were unaware. Moreover, there are many who have seen past and future lives upon reaching a high level of concentration during intense meditation in reliance upon the dharma. There are also many people who, because of previous instincts, recollect events from their former lives.

Therefore, as future birth certainly exists for us, we must establish a definite purpose for it now. The way to do this is to strive to become the embodiment of all good qualities; and, through constant familiarity with the noble path in past and future lives, or reliance upon a profound method in this very lifetime, sever the continuity of cyclic existence, so that the cycle of birth and death need be experienced no more.

CHAPTER 2

The History of Buddhism

●●●●●●●●●●●●

Homage to that perfect Buddha,
The supreme philosopher,
Who taught us dependent arising,
Free of destruction and creation,
Without annihilation and permanence,
With no coming and no going,
Neither unity nor plurality,
The quietening of fabrications,
The ultimate beatitude.

— Old scripture

The teacher of the Buddhist doctrine in this era was Gautama Buddha, who was born in the Shakya clan in India. Although he was born in a wealthy family, he sacrificed all worldly comforts, remaining in a remote area to practice, suffering great hardship. Only after that did he become fully enlightened.

According to the Kashmiri Pandit Sakya Sri, who came to Tibet in the early thirteenth century, the Buddha was born in India about 2,500 years ago. Despite conflicting assertions regarding the historical reckoning of his birth, there is a general consensus in literature about the key events of the Buddha's life. We know that the Buddha was originally an ordinary person like ourselves, with all the basic faults and weaknesses of a human being. He was born into a royal family, married and had a son. Later, however, he came into contact with the unsatisfactory suffering- nature of life in the form of unexpected encounters with people afflicted by sickness, old age and death. Deeply disturbed by these sights, the prince eventually left the palace and renounced his comfortable and sheltered princely way of life. His initial reaction to these experiences was to adopt the austere lifestyle of an ascetic, engaging in a spiritual path involving great physical penance. Later, he discovered that the true path out of suffering lies in a middle way — between the extremes of strict asceticism and self-indulgent luxury. His single-minded spiritual pursuit ultimately resulted in the full awakening of enlightenment: Buddhahood.

Over a period of millennia, the Indian Buddhist civilisation profoundly influenced all the other civilisations of Asia. Eventually, Buddhism was lost in India; and the twentieth century has seen its disappearance from much of the rest of Asia as well. But in the seventh century CE, Tibetan civilisation opened itself in a unique way to receive the great treasures of Indian Buddhism and, over the next thirteen centuries, the Tibetan people became more and more devoted to it, as it transformed their lives, land, society and deepest hearts.

Before Buddhism was brought from India to Tibet, the religion widespread in our country was the Bon belief. It had originated in the neighbouring country called Shang-Shung and, until recently, there were still centres in Tibet where the followers of the Bon faith pursued deep study and meditation. In its beginning, I believe, it was not a very fruitful religion, but when Buddhism took root and began to flourish in Tibet, it also benefited Bon — by enriching its religious philosophy and meditation techniques.

It was King Lha-Tho Ri Nyen-Tsen of Tibet who first introduced Buddhism to the country, well over a thousand years ago. Buddhism spread steadily and, in the course of time, many renowned scholars from India came to Tibet and translated the Sutra and Tantra texts and their commentaries.

This activity suffered a setback for some years during the reign of the irreligious King Lang-Dar-Mar in the tenth century of the Christian calendar; but that temporary eclipse was soon dispelled, and Buddhism revived and spread again, starting from the eastern and western parts of Tibet. Soon, distinguished scholars — both Indian and Tibetan — were busy once more in translating religious work, even if it meant journeying to Tibet. However, as Tibet again began to give birth to eminent native scholars, the number of scholars who came to Tibet from India and Nepal began to diminish gradually.

Thus, in what may be called the later period of Buddhism in Tibet, our religion developed separately from the later school of Indian Buddhism. But it retained the exact basis of the teachings of Lord Buddha. In its essentials, it never suffered alterations or additions at the hands of Tibetan lamas. Their commentaries are clearly distinguishable as commentaries and, for their authority, they referred to the main teachings of Lord Buddha or the works of Indian scholars.

Buddhism, as we have seen, was not brought to Tibet all at once; different scholars introduced scriptures at different times. In India, during that period, there were great Buddhist institutions, like the Nalanda and Vikramshila Universities, which differed slightly in their styles of teaching, although they taught the same fundamental religion and philosophy. Because of this, different groups grew into separate organisations or sects, which nevertheless had the same basic tenets. The most prominent of these Tibetan schools are Nyingma, Kagyu, Sakya and Geluk. Each of them adheres to all the teachings of Hinayana and Mahayana, including Tantrayana—for Tibetan Buddhists do not separate these teachings, but pay equal respect to them all. For moral guidance, they conform to the vinaya rules, which are principally followed by Hinayanists; while, for more esoteric practices, of every degree of profundity, they use the methods of the Mahayana and Tantrayana schools.

Who is the Buddha? The Buddha is a being who has attained complete purification of mind, speech and body. According to certain scriptures, the Buddha's mind, the Dharmakaya, or the Truth Body, can be taken as the Buddha. The Buddha's speech or inner energy can be taken as Dharma, the doctrine. And the Buddha's physical form can be taken as the Sangha, the spiritual community.

Is the Buddha permanent? Is Shakyamuni, an individual Buddha, eternal? No. Initially, Shakyamuni Buddha was Siddhartha, an ordinary being troubled by delusions and engaging in harmful thoughts and wrong actions — a person like us. However, with the help of teachings and teachers, he gradually purified himself and, in the end, became enlightened. Through the same causal process, we too can become fully enlightened.

CHAPTER 3

The Basic Tenets of Buddhism

• • • • • • • • • • • • • • • •

Like earth and the great elements
And also vast as the immensity of space,
Let me be the living ground
Of love for innumerable beings.

— Old scripture

Buddhist teachings are extremely profound as well as varied. Some say that Buddhism is not a religion, but rather a science of mind; and some say that Buddhists are atheists. In any case, Buddhism is a rational, deep and sophisticated approach to human life, which does not emphasise something external; rather, it emphasises personal responsibility for inner development. Buddha said, "You are your own master; things depend upon you. I am a teacher and, like a doctor, I can give you effective medicine, but you have to take it yourself and look after yourself."

There are two major schools of Buddhism: Mahayana, which translates as the greater vehicle; and Hinayana, the lesser vehicle. The system of the lesser vehicle was propounded by the Buddha in public teachings. Teachings of the greater vehicle were given to groups of people who were already disciples. The latter teachings include techniques for training the mind, as well as Tantrayana, or techniques for working with the vital energies and centres of the body. Buddhism, as observed and practised by the people of Tibet for many centuries, is complete — comprising all three levels of teachings.

The Sanskrit word 'Buddha' indicates a being whose mind is purified of faults and one whose realisation is completely developed. Buddha is also known as 'the one who has entered into the nature of suchness and the one who arose from it'.

To explain the meaning of a being arising from the nature of suchness, it is important to talk about the three bodies of a Buddha: the Truth Body (Dharmakaya), the Enjoyment Body (Sambhogakaya), and the Emanation Body (Nirmanakaya). Detailed explanations of the three bodies of the Buddha can be found throughout Mahayana literature.

According to this doctrine, when the Buddha came into this universe as Buddha Shakyamuni, he assumed the Emanation Body from the Truth Body. Here, all the great events in the life of the Buddha, from conception in the womb up to his Parinirvana, are regarded as deeds of the Buddha.

The Buddhas are also known as Gone to Bliss (Sugata), the ones who have passed into peace, have traveled the peaceful path into a peaceful state. This term includes peaceful realisations, peaceful abandonment or cessation, and the Buddha nature — the essence of the Buddha that, according to Buddhist doctrine, is inherent in all sentient beings.

Generally, the body, speech and mind of the Buddhas are explained as having different manifestations: the Body as Avalokiteshwara, speech as Manjushri, and mind as Vajrapani. Avalokiteshwara and Manjushri appear as peaceful deities, whereas Vajrapani looks slightly wrathful.

The Buddha always emphasised a balance of wisdom and compassion—a good brain and a good heart should work together. All beings have this subtle consciousness within them and, through the practice of deep meditation and virtuous actions, it can gradually be transformed into pure Buddhahood. The seed of liberation is within us.

To be good followers of the Buddha, the practice of compassion and honesty is essential. Showing kindness to others, we can learn to be less selfish; sharing the sufferings of others, we will develop more concern for the welfare of all living beings. This is the basic teaching. To implement this, we practice deep meditation and cultivate wisdom and, as our wisdom develops, our sense of ethics naturally grows stronger. There are many different levels of mind, the most subtle of which is the deep Buddha-nature, the seed of Buddhahood.

Placing importance just on the intellect, and ignoring the heart, can create more problems and more suffering in the world. On the other hand, if we emphasise only the heart and ignore the brain, then there is not much difference between humans and animals. They must be developed in balance and, when they are, the result is material progress accompanied by good spiritual development. Heart and mind working in harmony will yield a truly peaceful and friendly human family.

According to Buddhist scriptures, the creator of the world, as we know now, is nothing other than the ripening force of our own previous deeds, or karma. Every action establishes an imprint on the mind that contributes to our future evolution. Happiness is always a product of creative activity, and suffering of negative activity. Moreover, negative actions arise solely as a result of a deluded mind and positive actions as a result of a positive mind. Therefore, the aim of all religious practice is to cultivate and strengthen positive, creative states of mind and to eliminate negative, destructive states. A mind thus cultivated is both disciplined and calm; it gives peace to the person who possesses it, as well as to all with whom it comes in contact.

Efforts to actually realise the characteristic conditions of the Three Gems should be made during this life. And, for this, one must practise the Three Moral Precepts (the Trishiksha).

The Three Moral Precepts are:

1. Adishila Shiksha (Training in Higher Conduct)

2. Adisamadhi Shiksha (Training in Higher Meditation)

3. Adiprajnya Shiksha (Training in Higher Wisdom)

To use an analogy, Adishila Shiksha is the strength of a person, Adisamadhi his sure hand, and Adiprajnya his sharp axe. Using his sure hand, backed by his virile strength, he chops the wood (symbolising the notion of a permanent self and the defilement of sin being cut into pieces).

Training in Higher Conduct

The First Moral Precept, Adishila Shiksha, the foundation of the Three Moral Precepts, has many aspects. All these aspects are based on the precept that one must abandon the Ten Immoralities. Of the Ten Immoralities, three pertain to bodily action, four to the activity of speech, and three to the functioning of the mind.

The three immoralities pertaining to the body are:

1. The taking of the life of any living being—ranging from men to the smallest insect, whether directly or indirectly.

2. Stealing or taking another's property without consent, directly or indirectly, whatever its value.

3. Committing adultery and indulging in perverted forms of sexual intercourse.

The four immoralities pertaining to speech are:

1. Being guilty of falsehood, by leading others astray with false or wrong advice or information, and through all types of gestures or physical indications.

2. Being guilty of calumny, by causing disunity where unity exists and by aggravating disunity where disunity already exists.

3. The use of harsh and abusive language.

4. Indulgence in gossip-mongering out of sheer lust and passion.

The three immoralities pertaining to the functioning of the mind are:

1. Covetousness, or the desire to possess things that belongs to others.

2. The desire to harm others.

3. Heresy related to disbelief in rebirth, the Law of Causation and Effect and the Three Refuges

The antitheses of the Ten Immoralities are the Ten Virtues. When one practices the Ten Virtues, one is actually practicing Adishila Shiksha, or Higher Conduct.

A basic Buddhist standpoint is that, because the mind is essentially an entity of sheer luminosity and knowing, it can be shown that the mind can eventually know everything. From a philosophical viewpoint, this supports the position that good attitudes can be increased limitlessly.

CHAPTER 4

Dual Truth
• • • • • • • • • • • • •

E very religious path has a system of knowledge or Wisdom (Prajna) and Method (Upaya).

Wisdom relates to Absolute Truth (Paramarthasatya) and method to Relative Truth (Sambrithsatya). Nagarjuna has said: "The dharmas revealed by the Buddhas are always fully in accordance with the Dual Truths, both Absolute and Relative Truths."

When the final end of Buddhahood is achieved, an individual acquires two forms of Buddha or Bodies. These are the effects of his practice of Wisdom and Method in following the doctrinal paths; and his Wisdom and Method are the results of the two truths which are universally valid. An understanding of the Dual Truths is, therefore, very important, but there are some difficulties. Different schools of Buddhist thought hold divergent views.

According to Uma Thal Gyurpa (the theory of Madhyamika held by the Prasangika School of Buddhism) the things we perceive through our senses are of two aspects—the perceptible and the imperceptible. Generally speaking, Relative Truth is concerned with the knowledge of things, and of mental concepts in their perceptible aspects; and Absolute Truth with knowledge of their imperceptible aspects.

Objects of knowledge, taken as the basic category, can be divided into two classes — conventional and ultimate truths. When an object is directly perceived as being an ultimate truth, it ceases unequivocally to be a conventional truth. The same also applies to the perception of conventional truth and, therefore, the two truths are mutually exclusive. If either of the two truths did not exist, all objects of knowledge could not be classified within them, yet there is no third truth, which is not one of these two. Thus, the very mode of classification (into two truths) does not allow the possibility of a third category.

The two truths are distinct; nevertheless, if they were not one in nature, four absurd consequences would occur. A form's lack of true existence would not be that form's mode of being. Although a form's lack of true existence is realised, that realisation does not overcome grasping at signs (of its true existence). If it did, it would be meaningless for a yogi to meditate on higher paths. Even the Buddha has not burst the bonds of grasping at signs (of true existence); nor abandoned all the defilements, which result in bad states of birth.

If the two truths were one and indistinguishable even in their isolates, these absurd consequences would ensue. As both actions and delusions, which are by nature conventional misconceptions, are eliminated, the ultimate reality of phenomena would similarly be eliminated. Like conventional phenomena, ultimate reality would also have many different aspects. Even ordinary people would perceive ultimate reality directly and, while remaining an ordinary person, one would abandon all obscurations and become fully enlightened. Therefore, the two truths are one in nature but distinct in their isolates.

Ultimate truth is the actual object found by a reasoning consciousness analysing ultimate reality. The mind that is involved with worldly terms and designations is called a conventional mind, or a mind that is conventional, and the actual object found by it is a conventional truth.

In Sanskrit, ultimate truth is called paramartha satya; 'parama' means ultimate, excellent; 'artha' means purpose or meaning; 'satya' means truth, permanent. However, in this context, purpose does not denote the so-called purpose of self and others, but the objects understood by an exalted wisdom awareness, the object of analysis, the object to be found. It is called ultimate because it is excellent, exalted and bears such significance. Unlike conventional fictions, whose modes of appearance are incongruent with their mode of existence, it is, therefore, called truth or ultimate truth. If ultimate truth is further categorised, as Acharya Chandrakriti says in his supplement to Nagarjunas:

This selflessness was taught in two categories,

That of persons and that of phenomena,

In order to thoroughly liberate wandering beings.

Therefore, the Teacher further taught

Many aspects of it openly to the disciples;

Thus elaborating, he taught sixteen emptinesses

And abbreviating them again taught four,

Which are also accepted by the Mahayana.

So, both the selflessness of persons and the selflessness of phenomena may also be classified more elaborately as the four emptinesses. The emptiness of functional objects, the emptiness of functionless objects, the emptiness of nature and the emptiness of other entities. As the sixteen emptinesses—internal emptiness, and so on. As the eighteen emptinesses. And as the twenty emptinesses. All extant phenomena which are not emptinesses are known as conventional truths.

CHAPTER 5

Refuge in the Triple Gem

●●●●●●●●●●●●●●●●●●●

How can a worldly god,
Himself imprisoned in the jail of samsara,
Be able to protect anyone?
It is the practice of Bodhisattvas
To go for refuge to the Triple Gem,
Which will never deceive the person
Who takes refuge in it.

— Old scripture

The question can be asked, "What kind of refuge object is needed?" We are bound in the prison of cyclic existence and overpowered by karmic delusions. If we look at worldly kings, demigods, local gods or spirits, we will find many tales of the sufferings they inflict upon human beings. If they act positively, they can benefit us a little, but not significantly. If they are the kind of beings to whom humans feel they must make live animal sacrifices in order to avoid incurring their wrath, they are not worthy objects of refuge.

These gods and ghosts are similar to us in that they are overpowered by karma and other defilements. They lack the gross form of a body but resemble us in other respects. They are servants of the same three afflictions as us—

attachment, hatred and ignorance. So it makes no sense to seek refuge in gods, demigods and other beings who are subject to the same afflictions as we are.

We seek refuge because we look for the fulfilment of our expectations. Which object of refuge will never deceive us? There are three: the rare and supreme Buddha, the Dharma and the Sangha. To seek refuge from the very depths of our heart in the Triple Gem, appreciating it as the source of refuge through reasoning, is known as the practice of the Bodhisattvas.

That which we call the refuge is what distinguishes the Buddhist and the non-Buddhist. We become Buddhists when we trust the Triple Gem as the true source of refuge from the depths of our heart. Those who lack trust in the Triple Gem, and do not accept it as the proper source of refuge, are not necessarily Buddhists, even if they know many things about the Buddha dharma.

What is the nature of the Triple Gem — the Buddha, Dharma and Sangha? Buddha means one who is completely free from all faults, having destroyed them. The faults to be destroyed are not external but internal and, broadly speaking, we can say that all faults contained in the environment and migratory beings arise through the power of karma. This karma comes from the untamed mind and afflictions. These afflictions consist of any kind of thought which, when it arises, disturbs our mind and interferes with our inner peace. Therefore, to possess afflictions is to suffer; afflictions gain their name as a result of their mode of action.

Afflictions consist of both attachment and aversion, and the root of them all is ignorance allied with close-mindedness. Through the power of such afflictions, karma accumulates; and, through the power of ripened karma, sufferings are experienced. The principal afflictions, which need to be destroyed, are attachment, hatred and ignorance, as well as other mental negativity, including obscurations that prevent us from seeing the subtle nature of phenomena. Our minds become omniscient by overcoming all these hindrances. A person who is endowed with such qualities of mind is known as an Arya Buddha.

Even Buddha is neither permanent nor inherently existent. Nor do Buddhists believe that the Buddha was primordially enlightened, and that we sentient beings must remain forever in our current state. He who manifested the deeds of enlightenment at Bodhgaya was an ordinary being like us in the beginning. He became a Buddha by abandoning faults and generating good qualities step by step. Therefore, we also do not have to stay forever as sentient beings if we follow his example.

It is commonly believed in the world, and within the Hinayana view, that the Buddha was a Bodhisattva in his early life and attained enlightenment while sitting under the Bodhi tree in Bodhgaya. The Mahayana viewpoint is that all Buddhas never waver from the Dharmakaya and manifest different emanations that appear continuously, either gradually or suddenly, in the pure and impure realms. Among these manifestations was the fourth Buddha, Shakyamuni, who appeared in our world.

He was born as a prince in a royal family, was groomed to rule, but then took robes and became a monk. For six years, he practiced asceticism. Then, he overcame all obstacles and attained enlightenment. That he was enlightened for the first time, and had completely destroyed the defilements of dualistic delusion, was simply a manifestation.

The Buddha has the nature of the three kinds of body. Dharmakaya is the mind that views the two truths simultaneously and is also endowed with the two purities. The body that is endowed with Dharmakaya is the Subtle

Body and only appears to followers who are Arya beings. The Full Enjoyment Body, which is endowed with the Five Certainties, remains until cyclic existence empties. Such Supreme Emanation Bodies as Shakyamuni Buddha and Kashyapa Buddha appear from this Full Enjoyment Body.

The actual dharma has two aspects. The quality of abandonment, which in the supreme and precious dharma, includes everything from uprooting any false aspect of the mind to the truth of cessation, which is the complete eradication of the two obscurations in the mind of the Buddha. Then, there is the quality of realisation, which means understanding emptiness directly, the truth of the path. Those who are able to generate such qualities of realisation and abandonment become free from every single source of fear, and so the dharma can be seen as the true protector.

The Sangha comprises those who are endowed with the knowledge of abandonment and realisation. Thus the supreme Buddha, Dharma and Sangha are the objects of refuge for Buddhists. As proven protectors, the Buddha, Dharma and Sangha are presently separate from us and are the objects of our trust. Like a criminal trusting in his defence lawyer, our minds should seek the protection of these three by taking refuge in them.

What is involved in the process of seeking protection from the Triple Gem? Dispelling our faults and developing good qualities enables us to be free from suffering and to be endowed with a state of happiness. To achieve this, we must stop accumulating bad karma and create only good karma, by destroying the untamed delusional mind, which interferes with the accumulation of good karma, and the cessation of the development of bad karma.

The basis for dispelling all faults and generating good

qualities is the mind. When the positive qualities of the mind are developed, the faulty aspects lose power and eventually disappear. However if, during practice, the potential of the good qualities of mind decrease, the negative aspect will once again increase.

The support becomes firmer if we practise with the combination of method and wisdom and, as a result, the wholesome mind becomes stable and powerful. Because all these qualities are dependent upon the mind, they increase immeasurably when we practise and train in this manner continuously. Ultimately, we have to generate the truth of the path in our mental continuum. This is the supreme dharma. As a result, we attain the qualities of cessation of every single affliction of the mind. Then we will be free from suffering and will enjoy indestructible happiness.

Gradually, having developed our minds, we generate the wish to free ourselves from samsara, as well as the altruistic intention to help others. Similarly, little by little, we can discover the path of truth within ourselves with all its characteristics—seeing the nature of impermanence in objects, the nature of selflessness in phenomena and the nature of suffering in the afflictions of sentient beings. We create happiness and freedom from suffering by depending upon the path of cessation and of truth. Therefore, the dharma is known by Buddhists as the true refuge.

The precious Sangha is also very important as an example to be followed. According to Mahayana teachings, members of the actual precious Sangha have cultivated bodhichitta in their continuum and, supported by bodhichitta, have attained the union of calm abiding and special insight samadhi, by realising emptiness directly. Having attained the quality of the first ground and above, they are courageous and able to work successfully for the benefit of others. They have a marvellous inner strength, are endowed with immaculate knowledge and are invincible.

So we can see that the Buddha is the protector and is like a doctor; the precious dharma is the real protection and is like the medicine; and the spiritual Sangha is like a nurse, taking care of us like a good friend.

Those Bodhisattvas who are seeking the highest state of enlightenment in order to benefit others are practising the seeking of refuge in the Triple Gem.

CHAPTER 6

The Divisions of the Vehicles

Various systems of thought and practice are mentioned in classical Buddhist literature. Such systems are referred to as 'yanas' or vehicles. There are, for instance, the various vehicles of human and divine beings, in addition to the Buddhist vehicles—the vehicle of individual liberation (Hinayana), the vehicle of universal salvation (Mahayana), and the vehicle of Tantra (Vajrayana). In this context, vehicles of human and divine beings refer to systems that outline the essential training and methods for both fulfilling the major aspirations of this life and, in addition, obtaining a favourable rebirth as either a human or a divine being. Such systems emphasise the importance of leading an ethically sound life grounded in refraining from engaging in negative actions—since leading a life of righteousness and good behaviour are perceived to be the most crucial factors for ensuring a favourable rebirth.

The Buddha also spoke of another category of vehicle, the Brahma Vehicle, comprising principally those techniques of meditation that aim at achieving the highest possible form of life within samsara, the karmically-conditioned cycle of existence. Such meditative techniques include, among other things, withdrawing the mind from all external objects, which leads to a state of single-pointedness. The meditative states experienced as a result of having generated single-pointedness of mind are altered states of consciousness that, in terms of their phenomenological aspects and also their mode of engagement with objects, closely correspond to states of existence in form and the formless realms.

From the Buddhist point of view, all these diverse systems are worthy of respect, since they all have the potential to bring about great benefit to a large number of sentient beings. However, this does not mean that all these systems are complete in themselves in that they present a path leading to full liberation from suffering and from the cycle of existence. Genuine freedom and liberation can only be achieved when our fundamental ignorance, our habitual misapprehension of the nature of reality, is totally overcome. This ignorance, which underlies all our emotional and cognitive states, is the root factor that binds us to the perpetual cycle of life and death in samsara. This system of thought and practice, which presents a complete path towards liberation from this bondage, is called the vehicle of the Buddha (Buddhayana).

Within the Buddha's Vehicle there are two major systems of thought and practice: the Individual Vehicle, or Hinayana, and the Universal Vehicle, or Mahayana. In classical Buddhist literature, the Individual Vehicle is described as consisting of two main divisions: the Hearers' Vehicle and the Solitary Realisers' Vehicle. A principal difference between the Individual Vehicle and the Universal Vehicle lies in their views on the Buddhist doctrine of selflessness and the scope of its application.

The Individual Vehicle expounds the view of selflessness only in relation to things and events in general; whereas, in the Universal Vehicle, the principle of selflessness is not confined to the limited scope of the person, but encompasses the entire spectrum of existence, all phenomena. In other words, the Universal Vehicle system understands selflessness as a universal principle. Interpreted in this way, the principle of selflessness acquires greater profundity.

According to the Universal Vehicle teachings, it is only when a practitioner's experience of selflessness is rooted in this universal interpretation, that the experience will bring about the elimination of the delusions and their underlying states of ignorance. It is by eliminating these underlying states of ignorance that we are able to cut off the root of samsara.

Furthermore, a profound experience of selflessness can also lead, ultimately, to full enlightenment, a sense of total freedom from the subtle imprints and the obstructive habitual tendencies created by our misconception of the nature of reality. The system of thought and practice that presents such a view of selflessness is called Mahayana, the Universal Vehicle.

The Tantric Vehicle, or Vajrayana, which is considered by the Tibetan tradition to be the highest vehicle, is included within the Universal Vehicle. In addition to meditative practices that facilitate one's realisation of emptiness, this system also includes certain advanced techniques to utilise the various elements of the physical body in one's meditative practice.

Such feats are accomplished on the basis of sophisticated yogic practices that principally involve mentally penetrating the essential points within the body where the chakras, or energy centres, are located. By means of this subtle and refined coordination of mind and body, the practitioner is able to accelerate the process of getting at the root of ignorance and completely overcoming its effects and imprints—a process that culminates in the realisation of full enlightenment. This feature—of engaging in meditative practices involving the subtle coordination of both mental and physiological elements within the practitioner—is unique to the Tantric Vehicle.

CHAPTER 7

The First Turning of the Wheel of Dharma: The Four Noble Truths

● ●

A ccording to popular legend, following his full enlight-enment, the Buddha remained silent and did not give any teachings for forty-nine days. The first public teaching he gave was to the five ascetics who had been his companions when he was leading the life of a mendicant.

Having realised that asceticism does not lead to freedom from suffering, the Buddha—then called Siddhartha Gautama—had given up his penances and parted company with his fellows. His five companions had resented what they saw; they saw it as a betrayal and vowed never to associate with him. For them, this change in Siddhartha had indicated a failure to sustain his commitment to the life of asceticism.

However, when they met him after his enlightenment, they felt spontaneously drawn towards him. It was to these five former companions that the Buddha gave his first public teaching at Sarnath. In this discourse, which became known as the First Turning of the Wheel of Dharma, the Buddha taught the principles of the Four Noble Truths.

The root of the Buddhist doctrine is the four noble truths: true sufferings, sources, cessations, and paths. The four truths are two groups of effect and cause. Sufferings and their sources; and cessations of sufferings and the paths for actualising those cessations. Suffering is like an illness; the external and internal conditions that bring about the illness are the sources of suffering. The state of cure from the illness is the cessation of suffering and of its causes. The medicines that cure the disease are true paths.

The reason for this order with the effects of suffering and its cessation, before the causes and sources of suffering and paths, is this. Initially, one must identify the illness, true sufferings, the first noble truth. It is not sufficient to just to recognise the illness. In order to know which medicine to take, it is necessary to know the causes of the illness, the sources of suffering. This is the second noble truth.

Neither is it sufficient to just identify the causes of the illness; one needs to determine whether it is possible to cure the disease. Knowledge that reveals that it can be cured is similar to the third level, that of true cessation of suffering and its causes.

Now the unwanted suffering has been recognised; its causes have been identified; then, at the point at which it is understood that the illness can be cured, you take the medicines that are the means for removing the illness. Similarly, it is necessary to rely on the paths which will bring about the state of freedom from suffering.

It is considered most important, initially, to identify suffering. Suffering, in general, is of three types—the suffering of pain, the suffering of change and pervasive compositional suffering.

The suffering of pain is what we usually consider to be physical or mental suffering — for instance, a headache. The wish to be free from this type of suffering occurs not just in humans but also in animals. There are ways of avoiding some forms of this suffering, such as taking medicine, putting on warm clothes and moving away from the source.

The suffering of change is what we superficially consider to be pleasure but which, if we look into it, is actually suffering. Take, as an example, something usually considered to be pleasurable, such as buying a new car. When you first get it, you are very happy, pleased and satisfied—but then, as you use it, problems arise. As you begin to use it more and more, it begins to cause trouble. Therefore, such things are called sufferings of change; it is through change that their nature of suffering is revealed.

The third level of suffering serves as the basis for the first two, and is illustrated by our own contaminated mental and physical aggregates. It is called pervasive compositional suffering, since it pervades or applies to all types of transmigrating beings and is compositional in that it is the basis of present suffering and induces future suffering. There is no way of getting away from this type of suffering except by ending the continuum of rebirth.

What are the sources of these sufferings? In dependence on what does suffering arise? There are karmic sources and sources known as the afflictive emotions; these are the second of the four noble truths, true sources of suffering. For the cessation of karmas or actions that are a source of suffering, the cessation of afflictive emotions like obscuration, desire and hatred—which act as their cause— is necessary. Therefore, between karma and afflictive emotions, the main source of suffering is afflictive emotions.

When you question whether the afflictive emotions can be removed or not, you are concerned with the third noble truth: true cessations. If afflictive emotions resided in the very nature of the mind, it would be impossible to remove them. If hatred, for example, resided in the nature of the mind, then as long as we are conscious we should be hateful, but this is obviously not the case. Therefore, it is considered that the nature of the mind, of consciousness, is not polluted by defilements. The defilements are susceptible to being removed, capable of being separated from the basic mind.

It has been established that the sources of suffering can be gradually removed. With the utter extinction of the causes of suffering, there is true cessation. This is the final liberation; real, lasting peace; salvation. It is the third of the four noble truths.

In what kind of path should you train to achieve this cessation? Since faults mainly derive from the mind, the antidote must be generated mentally. Indeed, you need to know the final mode of subsistence of all phenomena, but it is most important to know the final status of the mind.

First, you need to realise directly, and in a totally non-dualistic manner, the final nature of the mind exactly as it is; this is called the path of seeing. Then, the next level is to become used to that perception; this is called the path of meditation. Before one comes to these levels, it is necessary to achieve a dualistic meditative stabilisation, which is a union of calm abiding and special insight. Prior to that, generally speaking, in order to have a powerful wisdom consciousness, it is necessary to first develop stability of mind, called calm abiding.

These are the levels of the path. The fourth noble truth, required for actualising the third noble truth, cessations that are states of having ceased the first two noble truths, sufferings and their sources. The four truths are intrinsic to the basic structure of Buddhist thought and practice.

CHAPTER 8

Karma

●●●●●●●●

Whatever joy there is in this world
All comes from desiring others to be happy.
And whatever suffering there is in this world
All comes from desiring my self to be happy.

— Shantideva

All of us desire happiness, the avoidance of suffering and of everything else that is unpleasant. Pleasure and pain arise from a cause, as we all know. Whether consequences are due to a single cause or to a group of causes is determined by the nature of those consequences. In some cases, even if the cause factors are neither powerful nor numerous, it is still possible for the effect factors to occur. Whatever the quality of the result factors, whether they are good or bad, their magnitude and intensity directly correspond to the quantity and strength of the cause factors. Therefore, to avoid unwanted pains and acquiring desired pleasures, which is in itself no small factor, the relinquishing of a great number of collective cause factors is required.

In analysing the nature and state of happiness, it will be apparent that it has two aspects. One is immediate joy (temporary); the other is deeper joy (ultimate). Temporary pleasures comprise the comforts and enjoyments which people crave—such as good dwellings, lovely furniture and so on. In other words temporary pleasures are what man enjoys in this life.

The question of whether the enjoyment of this pleasure and satisfaction derives purely from external factors, needs to be examined in the light of clear logic. If external factors alone were responsible for giving rise to such pleasures, a person would be happy when these were present and, conversely, unhappy in their absence. However, this is not so. Even in the absence of external conditions leading to pleasure, a man can still be happy and at peace.

This demonstrates that external factors are not solely responsible for creating man's happiness. Were it true that external factors were solely responsible, or that they wholly conditioned the arising of pleasure and happiness, a person possessing an abundance of these factors would have illimitable joy, which is by no means always so.

To say that these external factors are all that are needed, and are therefore the exclusive cause of happiness in a man's span of life, is an absurd and illogical proposition. It is by no means certain that the presence of such external factors will beget joy. On the contrary, factual happenings, such as the experiencing of inner fortitude and happiness, despite the local absence of such pleasure-causing external factors, as well as the frequent absence of joy despite their presence, clearly show that the cause of happiness depends upon a different set of conditioning factors.

If one were to be misled by the argument that the conditioning factors mentioned above constitute the sole cause of happiness, to the preclusion of any other conditioning causes, that would imply that (the resulting) happiness is inseparably bound to external causal factors, its presence or absence being exclusively determined by them. The fact that this is obviously not so is sufficient proof that external causal factors are not necessarily or wholly responsible for the effect phenomenon of happiness.

What is that other internal set of causes? How can it be explained? As Buddhists, we all believe in the law of karma, the natural law of cause and effect. Whatever external causal conditions someone comes across in subsequent lives result from the accumulation of that individual's actions in previous lives. When the karmic force of past deeds reaches maturity, a person experiences pleasant and unpleasant mental states. They are just a natural consequence of his previous actions.

The most important thing to understand is that, when suitable karmic conditions arising from the totality of past actions are present, one's external factors are bound to be favourable. The coming into contact of conditions, due to karmic action and external causal factors, will produce a pleasant mental state. If the requisite causal conditions for experiencing internal joy are lacking, there will be no opportunity for the occurrence of suitable external conditioning factors; or, even if these external conditioning factors are present, it will not be possible for the person to experience the joy that would otherwise be his.

This shows that inner causal conditions are essential— in that these conditions are what principally determine the experience of happiness (and its opposite). Therefore, in order to achieve the desired results, it is imperative for us to accumulate both the cause-creating external factors and the cause-creating internal (karmic) conditioning factors at the same time.

To state the matter in simple terms, for the accrual of good inner (karmic) conditioning factors, what is principally needed is qualities like having minimal wants, contentment, humility and simplicity. The practice of these inner causal conditions will even facilitate changes in the aforementioned external conditioning factors that will convert them into characteristics conducive to the arising of happiness.

The absence of suitable inner causal conditions such as having few wants, contentment, patience, forgiveness, and so on, will prevent one from enjoying pleasure, even if all the right external conditioning factors are present. Besides this, one must have to one's credit the force of merits and virtues accumulated in past lives. Otherwise, the seeds of happiness will not bear fruit.

It can be put in another way. The pleasures and frustrations, the happiness and suffering experienced by each individual are the inevitable fruits of beneficial and evil actions added to his store. If, at a particular moment in this present life, the fruits of a person's good actions ripen, he will recognise, if he is a wise man, that they are the fruits of (past) meritorious deeds. This will gratify him and encourage him to achieve more merit.

Similarly, when a person happens to experience pain and dissatisfaction, he will be able to bear them calmly if he maintains an unshakeable conviction that, whether he likes it or not, he must suffer and bear the consequences of his own (past) deeds. Besides, the realisation that they are nothing but the fruits of unskilled action in the past will make him wise enough to desist from unskilled deeds in the future. Likewise, the satisfying thought that, with the ripening of past (evil) karma, a certain part of the evil fruit borne by unskilled action in the past has been worked off, will be a source of immense relief.

Taking mind as the subject, and mind's ultimate reality as its object, one will properly comprehend the true essence of mind. After prolonged, patient meditation, one comes to perceive and grasp the knowledge of mind's ultimate reality, which is devoid of dual characteristics; then, one will be able to gradually exhaust the delusions and defects of the central and secondary minds—such as wrath, love of ostentation, jealousy, envy and so on.

As long as the mind is overwhelmed by wrong conceptions, there is no real peace. Life is lived in hallucination. Not seeing everything as illusory is the fundamental hallucination. The people who have not realised emptiness, and do not see things as illusory, not only see everything as truly existent, which is actually an illusion; they also experience the basic problem of clinging to everything as if it were true. This wrong conception, this ignorance, is the origin of all the other delusions that then motivate karma—the karma that leaves seeds in the mind, seeds that are the causes of samsara.

The ignorance of believing that everything exists on its own, ties you continuously to samsara; from life to life, you experience all the three types of suffering. It also interferes with your achieving liberation and enlightenment, and with your ability to fulfil the wishes of all sentient beings by leading them to the peerless happiness of full enlightenment.

Therefore, in your life, there is nothing to do other than to work for others, to cherish others, to rescue them from this ocean of misery, samsara, and establish them in the ultimate happiness of nirvana.

This inspiration creates a longing to devote one's energy to both the profound and extensive stages of the path of Mahayana. It is the root practice to accomplish Bodhisattva deeds, which connotes generosity, morality, patience, perseverance, meditation and wisdom. To be more precise, from the first three (generosity, morality and patience) stems the accumulation of virtue. From the last two (meditation and wisdom) stems the accumulation of sublime wisdom. And the fourth (perseverance) leads to both accumulations. In short, the key to the practice of Mahayana Buddhism in Tibet is dual coordination at every level, the coordination of virtue and wisdom, method and knowledge, Tantra and Sutra, relative and absolute.

Simultaneously, careful attention must be paid to the inherent moral implications of all the Buddha's teachings— desisting from harming others and cultivating the spirit of loving kindness. Viewed from the perspective of the bodhi mind, the goal is to maintain undiscriminating compassion towards all living beings, without making any distinction of race, nationality, class, tenuous status of friend or enemy.

In time, the great nations of the world, inspired by the Bodhimind, may cease to manipulate everything both sacred and profane, in a vain pursuit of power; instead, they will try to create a peaceful world, by regulating the mind's activities in accordance with dharma, the inexhaustible treasure.

Karma is not fatalistic or predetermined. Karma means our ability to create and to change. It is creative because we can determine how and why we act. We can change. The future is in our hands, and in the hands of our heart. Buddha said:

Karma creates all, like an artist
Karma composes, like a dancer.

The necessity of birth produced by karma ends only with the elimination of all karma. Karma will not end by itself, only by our awakening beyond all illusion. Then, the state of permanent happiness that comes from the total abandonment of ignorance will be attained. Therefore, the cessation of ignorance is liberation. Do not make the mistake of confusing nirvana with the end of all existence. We will continue to exist, but all karmic illusions will have dissipated, and this is the state of complete freedom and true happiness.

With regard to actions (karma) in general, there are two different systems of thought. One explains that any sort of karma is necessarily the mental factor of intention; another that says that there are also physical and verbal karmas. According to the first system, the mental factor of intention itself, at the time when it is initially motivating an action, is called an action of intention; whereas the mental factor of intention, at the time of actually engaging in the deed, is called an intended action. Thus, both are the mental factors of intention. According to the system that posits that there are also physical and verbal actions, actions of intentions are explained similarly, but intended actions occur at the point when the action is displayed physically.

Karma and its fruits can roughly be described as volitional action and its fruits—moral or psychological cause and effect. There are many methods of explaining the true nature of karma and its fruits. A generalised description would be, that all phenomena and objects are the results of causes. An effect is produced by a cause. Whether the result is good or bad depends upon the individual mind.

A negative cause and effect is indestructible and irrevocable. Take the example of a plant sapling. The effect, the plant sapling, comes into being because of its previous cause, the seed. The quality of an effect is dependent upon the quality of its corresponding cause. Similarly, pleasure and pain, or happiness and suffering, which are the lot of sentient beings, come from the individual's past causes — the law of cause and effect. The discovery that karma exists and is a fact and a reality, that it increases, that there is no fruit that is not conditioned by karma, and that nothing can hide from karma, is a truth of great significance.

Karma has four main characteristics. The first is its increasing effect: goodness heralds further goodness and evil creates more evil. The second is that karma is definite: in the long run, goodness always produces joy, and negativity always produces suffering. The third, that one never experiences a joy or sorrow that does not have a corresponding karmic cause. The fourth, that karmic seeds placed in the mind at the time of an action never lose their potency even in a hundred million lifetimes, but lie dormant until the conditions that activate them appear.

CHAPTER 9

Dependent Arising
●●●●●●●●●●●●●●●●●●●●●●●●●●●

Dependent arising is the general philosophy of all
Buddhist systems, even though there are many
different interpretations. In Sanskrit, the word used for
dependent arising is pratityasamutpada. The word 'pratitya'
has three different meanings—meeting, relying and
depending—but all three basically mean dependence.
'samutpada' means arising. Hence, the meaning of
'pratityasamutpada' is that which arises in dependence
upon conditions, in reliance upon conditions, through the
focus of conditions.

At a subtle level, it is the main reason why phenomena
are empty of inherent existence. In order to reflect on the
fact that things—the subjects on which a meditator reflects—
are empty of inherent existence because they are dependent
arisings, it is necessary to identify the subjects of this
reflection — the phenomena that produce pleasure and
pain, help and harm, and so forth. If one does not
understand cause and effect well, it is extremely difficult
to realise that these phenomena are empty of inherent
existence, because they are dependent arisings.

One has to understand the presentation of cause and
effect — they cause help and harm in certain ways because
there are the bases with respect to which emptiness is to
be realised, by understanding that they have dependently
arisen. Hence, Buddha set forth a presentation of dependent
arising in connection with the cause and effect of actions,

in the process of life in cyclic existence, so that penetrating understanding of the process of cause and effect could be gained.

Thus, there is one level of dependent arising that is concerned with causality — in this case the twelve branches, or links, of dependent arising of life in cyclic existence. Ignorance, action, consciousness, name and form, the six sense spheres, contact, feeling, attachment, grasping, existence, birth, ageing and death. Then there is a second, deeper level of dependent arising that applies to all objects—the establishment of phenomena dependent on their parts. There is no phenomenon that does not have parts, and thus every phenomenon is imputed in dependence upon its parts.

There is a third, even deeper level, which is the fact that phenomena are merely imputed by terms and conceptuality, in dependence upon their bases of imputation. There is nothing to be found that is the object imputed, and thus phenomena are merely dependently arisen—in the sense that they are imputed in dependence upon bases of imputation.

Whereas the first level of dependent arising refers to the arising of compounded phenomena in dependence upon causes and conditions, and thus applies only to impermanent or caused phenomena, the other two levels apply to both permanent and impermanent phenomena. When the Buddha set forth the twelve links of dependent arising, he spoke from a vast perspective and with great import. He taught the twelve links in detail in the Rice Seedling Sutra. As in other discourses, the context is one of questions that the Buddha answers. In this sutra, he speaks of dependent arising in three ways:

1. Due to the existence of this, that arises.

2. Due to the production of this, that is produced.

3. It is thus: due to ignorance there is compositional action; due to compositional action there is consciousness; due to consciousness there are name and form; due to name and form there are the six sense spheres; due to the six sense spheres there is contact; due to contact there is feeling; due to feeling there is attachment; due to attachment there is grasping; due to grasping there is the potentialised level of karma called existence; due to existence there is birth; and due to birth there are ageing and death.

When, in the first rendition, the Buddha says, "Due to the existence of this, that arises," he indicates that the phenomena of cyclic existence do not arise through the force of supervision by a permanent deity, but due to specific conditions. Merely due to the presence of certain causes and conditions, specific effects arise.

In the second phase, when the Buddha says, "Due to the production of this, that is produced," he shows that a produced, permanent phenomenon (such as the general nature propounded by the Samkhya system) cannot perform the function of creating effects. Rather, the phenomena of cyclic existence arise from conditions that are impermanent by nature.

Then, this question arises. If the phenomena of cyclic existence are produced from impermanent conditions, could they be produced from just any impermanent factors? This would not be sufficient. Thus, in the third phase, he indicates that the phenomena of cyclic existence are not produced from just any impermanent causes and conditions, but from specific ones that have the potential to give rise to specific phenomena.

Setting forth dependent arising, the Buddha shows that suffering has ignorance-obscuration as its root cause. This impure, faulty seed gives birth to an activity that deposits in the mind a potency that will generate suffering, by producing a new life in cyclic existence. Its eventual fruit is the last link of dependent arising, the suffering of ageing and death.

With regard to the twelve links of dependent arising, there are basically two modes of explanation, one in terms of thoroughly afflicted phenomena and another in terms of pure phenomena. In the four noble truths, which are Buddha's root teaching, there are two sets of cause and effect, one for the afflicted class of phenomena and another for the pure class. Here too, in the twelve links of dependent arising, there are procedures in terms of both afflicted phenomena and pure phenomena.

Among the four noble truths, true sufferings (the first truth) are effects in the afflicted class of phenomena, and true sources (the second truth) are their causes. In the pure class of phenomena, true cessations (the third truth) are effects in the pure class, and true paths (the fourth) are their causes.

Similarly, when it is explained in the twelve links of dependent arising that, due to the condition of ignorance, action is produced and so forth, the explanation is in terms of the afflicted procedure; and when it is explained that due to the cessation of ignorance action ceases, and so forth, it is in terms of the procedure of the pure class. The first is the procedure of the production of suffering, and the second is the procedure of the cessation of suffering.

Another mode of dependent arising is the establishment of phenomena in dependence upon their parts. Physical objects have directional parts, and formless phenomena, such as consciousness, have temporal parts — earlier and later moments that form their continuum. If there were things like part-less particles to serve as the building-blocks of larger objects, one could not discriminate, for instance, between its left and right sides or the front and the back. If you cannot discriminate between the sides of something then, no matter how many of them you put together, you would not have anything more than the size of the original one. It would be impossible for them to be amassed. However, the fact is that gross objects are produced through the coming together of many minute particles. Thus, no matter how small the particle is, it must have directional parts. Through this logic, it is established that there are no physical objects that are part-less.

Similarly, with respect to a continuum, if the smallest moments of a continuum did not have earlier and later parts themselves, there would not be any possibility of their coming together to form a continuum. If a moment had no parts, such that what was in contact with what precedes it was also equally in contact with what follows it, there would be no way for such part-less moments to form a continuum. Similarly, with respect to unchanging phenomena such as un-compounded space, there are parts or factors such as space in the eastern quarter and space in the western quarter, or the part associated with this object and the part associated with that object. Thus any object, whether it is impermanent or permanent, changing or unchanging, has parts.

However, when the whole and the parts of any object—the latter being that in dependence upon which the whole is imputed—appear to our minds, the whole appears to have its own separate entity and the parts appear to be parts. Is this not the case? Though they depend on each other, they seem to have their own entities. They appear to our conceptual thought in this manner, but if they did in fact exist this way, you should be able to point your finger at a whole that is separate from its parts.

Thus, you can see that there is a discrepancy between the way the whole and the parts appear and the way they actually exist—in that they seem to have their own separate entities, but actually do not. However, this does not mean there are no objects that are wholes, because if there were no wholes, you could not speak of something as being a part of anything, for the whole is that in relation to which something is posited as its part.

Hence, there are wholes, but their mode of existence is such that they are designated in dependence upon their parts—they do not exist in any other way. This applies not just to changing, impermanent phenomena but also to permanent, unchanging phenomena and is thus broader in meaning than the former interpretation of dependent arising, which is limited to phenomena arisen in dependence upon causes and conditions.

Thus, in the term 'dependent arising', 'dependent' means depending, or relying, on other factors. Once the object depends on something else, it is devoid of being under its own power—it is devoid of being independent. Hence, it is empty of an independent nature, of being under its own power. Nevertheless, it does arise in reliance upon conditions.

Good and bad, cause and effect, oneself and others— all objects are established in reliance upon other factors; they arise dependently. Due to being dependently arisen, objects are devoid of the extreme of being under their own power. Also because, in this context of dependence, help and harm arise and exist, objects do not not exist—their performance of functions is feasible. In this way, the causes and effects of actions are feasible, as is the 'I' that is their basis. When one understands this, one is released from the extreme of non-existence, nihilism.

Looked at like this, existing in dependence upon conceptuality is also a meaning of dependent arising—the subtlest meaning. These days, physicists explain that phenomena do not exist just objectively in and of themselves, but exist in terms of, or in the context of, involvement with a perceiver, an observer.

CHAPTER 10

Impermanence and Death

· · · · · · · · · · · ·

*It is the practice of Bodhisattvas to renounce
  this life,
Since relatives and friends of long-standing
  must part,
Wealth and material goods accumulated with
  great effort must be left behind,
And the body, like a guest house, must be
  discarded by the guest of consciousness.*
— Old scripture

We are true dharma practitioners if we seek a solitary
place and are able to renounce this worldly life. In
order to renounce worldly life, we should look upon this
life as essence-less—the ultimate reasons for such a view
being impermanence and death. All of us have to die
sooner or later. If we have practised dharma and developed
good-heartedness, at the time of death future circumstances
look hopeful. Otherwise, even if all the people of the world
were our friends and relatives, it would not benefit us at
such a time, because we must go alone, leaving all of them
behind. A very wealthy person, for example, who owns a
chain of factories, must leave all those factories behind
when he dies.

From the time we left our mother's womb, until now, we have cherished our bodies devotedly, but this doesn't benefit us in the end, because we must also leave this body behind. Even as far as the Dalai Lama is concerned, when the day of death comes, then of course he has to leave the body of Tenzin Gyatso. There is no way in which body and mind can go together. Usually, if deprived of his blessed robe (cho gos nam jar), Tenzin Gyatso will experience a downfall; but at the time of death one has to leave this holy robe behind without any downfall.

The time of our death is uncertain. Making plans would be worthwhile if we could trust in a fixed lifespan, but we cannot trust in the duration of our life because we don't know when we will die. We are all together here in this dharma session today, but some of us may die tonight. We cannot be sure that we will all meet again in tomorrow's session. I cannot give you a 100% guarantee that I won't die tonight, for example.

So, if we remain clinging to this life even for one day, we are misusing our time. In this way, we can waste months and years on end. Because we don't know when our lives will finish, we should remain mindful and well prepared. Then, even if we die tonight, we will do so without regret. If we die tonight, the purpose of being well prepared is borne out; if we don't die tonight, there is no harm in being well prepared, because it will still benefit us.

The physical activity of this lifetime may be observed and understood, and things have a way of working themselves out in time. For instance, we experienced a great deal of uneasiness and frustration when we first escaped from Tibet and came to India, wondering how we would survive. In this process of fleeing from one nation to another, we found that gradually everything worked out.

But when we leave the world of humans, we do so without a protector or supporter and the total responsibility falls on us. We only have our own intelligence to rely on at that time, so we must expend our own effort in order to protect ourselves. As the Buddha said, "I have shown you the path to liberation; know that liberation depends on you." We must put strenuous effort into gaining freedom from the lower migrations, liberation from samsara, freedom from conventional existence and solitary salvation.

It is difficult for the devas to protect us when we go to the next life, so we should be cautious and become as well prepared now as we can. We should place emphasis on future lifetimes, rather than clinging to this lifetime only, so that we are able to sacrifice or renounce this life. This is stated in order to establish the essence-less-ness of this life.

The body is compared to a guest house; it is a place to stay for just a short time and not permanently. At present, the guest of consciousness is staying in the guest house of the body, like renting a place to stay. When the day comes for consciousness to leave, the guest house of the body must be left behind. Not being attached to friends, the body, wealth and possessions is the practice of the Bodhisattvas.

CHAPTER 11

Rebirth

• • • • • • • •

A s Asanga says in his *Compendium of Manifest Knowledge*, there are two types of true sufferings—environments and the beings within them. The varieties of suffering within cyclic existence are included within three realms of cyclic existence — the Desire Realm, the Form Realm and the Formless Realm. The three realms are rough groupings of levels of cyclic existence, in terms of the fruits of three levels of consciousness, these being determined by levels of conceptuality.

Rebirth in the Formless Realm is an effect of the subtlest level of meditative stabilisation. Rebirth in the Form Realm is an effect of lower levels of meditative stabilisation. And rebirth in the Desire Realm, our realm, is an effect of a lower level of consciousness that has not reached such concentration.

Buddhists believe that the world is endless and that sentient beings are infinite in number. Therefore, some people ask, "If there is an endless number of sentient beings, isn't the generation of an intention to become enlightened for the sake of all sentient beings rather senseless?"

The answer to this is that the intention is very important. One must generate a good intention; whether one can actually achieve it or not is another matter. For instance, if a doctor generates great determination to rid the world of a certain illness and therefore engages in research, it would be good, wouldn't it? In terms of determination, will power, there is no limit. Whether practical or not, your decision—with strong determination right from the beginning—will carry weight. Whether it is achieved or not is a different question.

In terms of the levels of grossness and subtlety of mind, there are three realms and six types of transmigrating beings. However, according to Buddhism, beings do not achieve liberation by progressing higher and higher within these levels. When one arrives at the peak of cyclic existence, it is not as if one is at the threshold of liberation; it is still easy to fall back into lower states. Therefore, it is said that there is no definiteness with respect to the states of rebirth.

How does one pass from one birth state to another? First, we must discuss rebirth. The main reason that establishes rebirth is the continuation of mind. There are basically two types of phenomena — internal consciousness and external matter. Matter can serve as a cooperative cause for the generation of consciousness — such as when a material, visible object serves as a cause of a consciousness being produced in the aspect of that particular object. This is called an observed object condition.

However, matter cannot serve as the substantial cause of consciousness. To explain this, let us consider the three causal conditions that generate, for example, eye consciousness. The three are an empowering condition, observed object condition, and an immediately preceding condition. Each of the three conditions has a unique function. For instance, the fact that eye consciousness is able to perceive a visible form and not a sound is due to the eye sense power (a type of subtle, clear matter located in the organ of the eye) that is its empowering condition. That an eye consciousness is generated as having an aspect of, for example, blue and not yellow, is due to the patch of blue itself, which is its observed object condition. Also, that an eye consciousness is generated as an entity of luminosity and knowing is due to an immediately preceding moment of consciousness that serves as its immediately preceding condition.

Without a former continuum of consciousness, there is no way that it could be produced as an entity of luminosity and knowing. Therefore it is established that, without a preceding mind, a later mind cannot be produced. In this way, it is also established that there is no beginning to consciousness, and in the same way there is no end to the continuum of a person's consciousness.

The quality of one's rebirth in the next life is determined by the quality of one's mental activity in this one. Generally speaking, we have no power to choose how we are born; it is dependent on karmic forces. However, the period near the time of death is very influential in terms of activating one from among the many karmas that a person has already accumulated and, therefore, if one makes particular effort at generating a virtuous attitude at that time, there is an opportunity to strengthen and activate a virtuous karma. Moreover, when one has developed high realisation and gained control over how one will be reborn, it is possible to take what is called reincarnation rather than mere rebirth.

How does one go from lifetime to lifetime? When one dies from either the Desire Realm or the Form Realm to be reborn in the Formless Realm, there is no intermediate state; otherwise, whenever one takes rebirth, there is an intermediate state between this life and the next life. What is the mode of procedure of death and what is the nature of the intermediate state? First, dying can take place upon the exhaustion of merit, or from an accident. According to the very coarse explanation of death in Vasubandhu's *Treasury of Manifest Knowledge,* the mind of death itself can be virtuous as can even the first moment of conception. In this case, a virtuous mind of death can act as an immediately preceding condition causing a virtuous mind of conception of the next life. However, Asanga's *Compendium of Manifest Knowledge* sets forth a more subtle presentation, in which the mind of death is necessarily neutral, as is the mind of the first moment of rebirth. In addition, in Highest Yoga Mantra, there is a presentation of far subtler levels of consciousness, which can be utilised such that a person who has practised Highest Yoga Mantra well can transform even the subtlest mind of clear light of death into a virtuous consciousness.

In general, those who have steadfastly practiced virtue during their lifetime have an easier and more peaceful death, whereas those who have engaged in many non-virtuous activities have a more difficult and more agitated death.

During the process of death, the warmth of the body withdraws from parts of the body in different ways for different types of people. For those who have accumulated a great deal of virtuous karma, the warmth of the body initially withdraws from the lower portion of the body, whereas for those who have accumulated a great deal of non-virtuous karma, the warmth initially withdraws from the upper portions of the body. Then, stage by stage, the outer breath ceases, and the warmth gathers at the heart.

According to the system of Highest Yoga Mantra, the process of death is presented in terms of the four or five elements. In this explanation, the capacity of the elements to serve as bases to consciousness gradually diminishes, thereby producing a series of mental appearances. When the capacity of the earth element to serve as a basis of consciousness deteriorates, as an external sign the body becomes thinner, and so on. As an internal sign, in accordance with the explanation of the Guhyasamaja system, you have a sense of seeing a mirage. Then, when the capacity of the water element to serve as a basis of consciousness deteriorates, your tongue dries, and your eyes sink into your head. As an internal sign, you have a sense of seeing smoke. Then, when the capacity of the fire element to serve as a basis of consciousness deteriorates, the warmth of your body gathers, as explained above. As an internal sign, you have a sense of seeing fireflies. Then, when the capacity of the wind or air element to serve as a basis of consciousness deteriorates, your breath ceases and, as an internal sign, you have a sense of seeing a burning butter lamp in space in front of you. Earlier, there was an appearance of fireflies or of sparks from a fire; this now disappears, and a reddish type of appearance occurs.

Then, the subtler levels of the winds, or inner airs, that serve as the mounts of consciousness, begin to dissolve. First, the winds that serve as the mounts of the eighty conceptions dissolve to a mind called appearance, during which there is a vivid white appearance; this is the first of four states called the four emptinesses. Then, when the mind of vivid white appearance — as well as the wind or inner energy that serves as its mount — dissolves into the mind called increase of appearance, there is a vivid red or orange appearance. Then, when the mind of vivid red increase of appearance, as well as the wind that serves as its mount, dissolves into the mind called near-attainment, there is an appearance of blackness. If doctors happened to be present at this time, they would probably have already declared you dead; however, in terms of this explanation, a person has not died, but is dying. Then, after the vivid black near-attainment, the mind of clear light of death dawns. This consciousness is the innermost subtle mind. We call it the Buddha nature, the real source of all consciousness. The continuum of this mind lasts even through Buddhahood.

While the clear light of death is manifesting, the consciousness is still inside the body. Then, simultaneous with the cessation of the mind of clear light of death, mind and body separate. This is the final farewell!

Simultaneous with the separation of mind and body, one passes through the same set of eight appearances in reverse order. If there is an intermediate state, it begins with the reappearance of the mind of vivid black near-attainment.

What is the nature of an intermediate state? A being of the intermediate state does not have a gross physical body like ours, but a subtle body. It is achieved just from the winds (inner airs) and mind. Hence, wherever the intermediate state being feels like going, the body of that person immediately arrives there.

What is the physical shape of a being in the intermediate states? About this, there are two discordant presentations. According to Vasubandhu and certain mantric texts, the body of an intermediate state being resembles that of the being as whom he or she will be reborn. With respect to how long one spends in the intermediate state, a single lifespan in the intermediate state is, at the most, seven days, at the end of which there is a small death, and the longest period one can stay in such a series of intermediate states is seven weeks — forty-nine days. However, there are two different ways of calculating how long a day is; one system posits them in terms of human days, and the other in terms of the type of life into which one will be reborn.

What kinds of perception does an intermediate state being have? In accordance with the good and the bad karma (deeds) of the person, various favourable and unfavourable appearances occur. Also, one can see other beings of one's own level. Moreover, Vasubandhu's *Treasury of Manifest Knowledge* says that persons who have achieved, through effort, the clairvoyance of the divine eye, can see beings in the intermediate state. Just after one leaves one's old body and emerges into an intermediate state, one can indeed see that old body; however, in general, one has no wish to get back into it. Still, in some cases, persons have re-entered the old body; it is possible — if the karmic circumstances are present — to revive the old body. In Tibetan, this is called *day lok*, "returning from having passed away."

The intermediate state being makes a connection to a new birth and, in general, four types of birth are described— spontaneous birth, birth from a womb, birth from an egg, and birth from heat and moisture. An intermediate state being is a case of spontaneous birth. It is also said that, when this world system formed, beings were born here spontaneously, fully developed. If the rebirth is to be from heat and moisture, one sees a pleasant, warm place to which one becomes attached such that one has a wish to stay there. If one is to be reborn by way of womb-birth, one sees the father and mother in copulation. Those to be reborn as males are attracted to and desire the mother; those to be reborn as females are attracted to and desire the father; during such desire, the intermediate state stops and the birth state begins.

Cessation of the intermediate state and conception in the mother's womb are simultaneous. In the process of the cessation of the intermediate state, one passes through the eight signs — beginning with the sense of mirage, as explained earlier, at the end of which the mind of clear light dawns. Because the body of an intermediate state being is subtle, these eight signs are not clear and occur quickly, whereas because our type of body is gross, the eight signs are clear and last a longer period of time. Due to this fact, it is said that, for a person who wishes to practice Highest Yoga Tantra, a human birth is very favourable.

This is the way we travel, seemingly endlessly, in cyclic existence. As long as we are in such cyclic existence, we undergo many different types of suffering.

CHAPTER 12

The Second Turning: The Doctrine of Emptiness

• • • • • • • • • • •

Know all things to be like this:
A mirage, a cloud castle,
A dream, an apparition,
Without essence, but with qualities that can be
  seen.

Know all things to be like this:
As the moon in a bright sky
In some clear lake reflected,
Though to that lake the moon has never moved.

Know all things to be like this:
As an echo that derives
From music, sounds, and weeping,
Yet in that echo is no melody.

Know all things to be like this:
As a magician makes illusions
Of horses, oxen, carts and other things,
Nothing is as it appears.

— The Buddha

In the Second Turning of the Wheel of Dharma at Vulture's Peak, the Buddha taught the Wisdom Sutras — the collection of sutras known as Perfection of Wisdom (Prajnaparamita). These sutras focus primarily on the topics of emptiness and the transcendent states associated with the experience of emptiness. The second turning should be seen as expanding upon the topics that the Buddha taught in the first turning of the wheel.

The theory of shunyata, or emptiness, is common ground for all the four main schools of Buddhist thought. However, the most perfect and excellent description of the meaning of shunyata, profound and vast as it is, can be found only in the Mahayana schools of Buddhist thought, which is regarded as the principal school among the four. The term shunyata, or voidness, does not mean that there is nothing, that nothing exists, like describing a flower called sky-flower that does not exist at all. Shunyata is attributeless, but implies that whatever is born of a cause exists; yet exists only in relation to, or dependent upon, something other than itself. Its origination is not origination in fact: that is shunya. Things are simply mental designations and nothing else. They are non-self-existing. All objects are shunya by nature. They are void. They are empty of permanent substance or self because they are non-self-existing, being dependent upon causes other than themselves. But this does not mean that objects do not exist at all.

The 'I' (self) is a denomination named in relation to the aggregates (groups of physical and mental properties dependent on grasping). It is generally believed that the 'I' (self) and aggregates each have their own separate existence. However, Buddhists recognise and identify the nature of the self and the aggregates as being related. The 'I' depends upon the aggregates for its existence. For instance, a chariot is the name given to its different parts collectively. Similarly, it is possible for us to speak of the self or 'I' only in relation to the aggregates. To quote the words of the Master: "A chariot is named as such in relation to the cohesive whole of its different parts. Likewise, a relative living being is just a name designated in relation to the collectiveness (cohesive wholeness) of the aggregates."

All the four main schools of Buddhist thought freely subscribe to this point of view, in spite of the fact that the approach adopted by each school in explaining the nature of the conditioned 'I' is quite different. Of the four schools, Madhyamika is considered the most important. Madhyamika is again divided into two sub-schools: Prasangika and Sautantrika. According to the Prasangika sub-school, the self or 'I' is a mere name as construed by comprehension. Just as the self is a mere name as construed by comprehension, all objects are mere names as construed by comprehension. All objects are non-self-existent — they do not have an existence of their own.

According to the explanation of the highest Buddhist philosophical school, Madhyamika-Prasangika, external phenomena are not mere projections or creations of the mind. External phenomena have a distinct nature, which is different from the mind. The meaning of all phenomena has a distinct nature, which is different from the mind. The meaning of all phenomena being mere labels or designations is that they exist and acquire their identities by means of our denomination or designation of them. This does not mean that there is no phenomena apart from the name, imputation or label. Phenomena are unable to withstand such analysis; therefore, they do not exist objectively. Yet, since they exist, there should be some level of existence; therefore, it is only through our own process of labeling or designation that things are said to exist.

Since phenomena have no independent, objective reality, there is no status of existence from the viewpoint of the object; therefore we conclude that phenomena exist only nominally, or conventionally. However, when things appear to us, they do not appear as mere designations; rather they appear to us as if they have some kind of objective reality or inherent existence. Thus, there is a disparity between the way things appear to us and the way they exist. This is why they are said to be illusory.

The actual mode of existence of phenomena can be ascertained only through your own experience, once you have negated their inherent existence. But conventional reality cannot be logically proved. For example, this table exists because we can touch it, feel it, put things on it, and so on; thus, it exists. It is only through our direct experience of a phenomenon that we can establish the reality of its existence.

The Prasangika sub-school speaks of three criteria that determine whether or not something is existent: it should be known through a worldly convention; such a convention should not be contradicted by any form of validation; and it should not be contradicted by an ultimate analysis of its nature. Anything possessing these three criteria is said to be conventionally existent.

Let us consider, for example, present time. It is definite that the present exists, but let us examine what it is in greater depth. We can divide time: the time that is gone is the past, and the time that is yet to come is the future. If we divide time even more minutely, we will find that there is hardly anything remaining that we can truly call present. We find that between the past and the future there is an extremely thin line — something that cannot really withstand analysis and remain as the present. If we were to maintain a single point in time as indivisible, then there would be no grounds for dividing between the past, present and future, because it would all be indivisible. But when we speak of divisible time, then there is hardly any present remaining between the past and future.

If the present cannot be posited, how can past and future be posited? Past is called past in relation to the present, and future is called future in relation to the present as well. If we were to conclude that the present does not exist, this would contradict worldly convention and our everyday thought and experience as well as many other facts. Therefore we say that the present does exist, but not inherently or objectively.

CHAPTER 13

Mahayana

• • • • • • • • • • • • •

Just like space
And the great elements such as earth
May I always support the life
Of all the boundless creatures.

— Old scripture

Buddha's teachings included both Hinayana and Mahayana;
the Mahayana is greater in its motivation, its practices
and its objective. Its motivation is that of happiness for all
sentient beings, instead of just one's own well being. The
practice of six or ten paramitas accompanies the Mahayana.
And the goal of this teaching includes not only liberation
from samsara, but also attainment of the three kayas:
Nirmanakaya, Sambhogakaya and Dharmakaya.

The Mahayana dharma includes the paths of Paramitayana
and Vajrayana. The latter has different qualities that make
it superior to the sole practice of the paramitas, but the
union of both is very important. During Gautama Buddha's
lifetime, the Hinayana flourished, because it was easy to
comprehend and could therefore be taught to numerous
listeners. The Mahayana, which demanded a better-prepared
mind was less popular and was taught only to advanced
disciples. This is why it was criticised and its existence in
early Buddhism was contested and still is, by some people.

However, the Mahayana really existed from the very
beginning in Gautama Buddha's First Turning of the Wheel

of Dharma. After the Parinirvana, it seems to have disappeared for several centuries. The Mahayana had a resurgence at the time of Nagarjuna.

Nagarjuna was the restorer of the Mahayana. His coming had been prophesied by the Buddha in several sutras, particularly the Manjushri Multantra. Nagarjuna lived about four hundred years after the Buddha. From his time, the Mahayana underwent a great expansion, then renewal, several centuries after it had degenerated. The practice, the method of the Tibetan Mahayana, and its teaching, unifies the Sutras and Tantras aimed at cultivating Bodhichitta. The aspiration of Bodhichitta is the realisation of shunyata.

What Mahayana Buddhism teaches is this: from the very core of our heart, we should sacrifice our life, possessions and merit for the sake of other sentient beings, as we find in Shantideva's *A Guide to the Bodhisattva's Way of Life*:

> *When both myself and others*
> *Are similar in that we wish to be happy*
> *What is so special about me?*
> *Why do I strive for my happiness alone?*
> *And when both myself and others*
> *Are similar in that we do not wish to suffer*
> *What is so special about me?*
> *Why do I protect myself and not others?*

Although we all desire happiness and do not want suffering, we are still under the sway of the three root delusions and are unable to help either ourselves or anyone else. This pathetic situation is the unfortunate result of our selfish outlook and, therefore, all of us should endeavour to generate a good heart. Bringing about the welfare of others is being absolutely flawless, from start to finish, temporarily and permanently, being neither flattering nor backbiting. Whoever we are, if we are able to cultivate such a good heart, we will not only be flawless ourselves, but we will receive inconceivable benefits. So should we not generate such a noble thought? If we are able to do so, not only will each of us enjoy happiness, even in this life, but those around us will enjoy peace and quiet too.

So, all of us should try our best to cultivate a good heart towards others and give up selfish motives. In this, the dharma is in accordance with the ways of the world; it brings happiness to self and others both temporarily and ultimately, and nothing is superior to this.

The essential point of the Mahayana teaching is to help others, while the essential point of the Hinayana teaching is not to harm others. These two phrases "help others if possible" and, "if not, do not harm them" between them condense the meaning of all the eighty-four thousand heaps of Buddha's teaching.

There is no benefit in such profound instructions without that foundation, even though there may be the generation and completion stages, channels winds and drops, and so on. We have to turn into a proper vessel to receive the teachings, just as we must be able to stand up to strong medicine prescribed for us and not have too weak a constitution to tolerate it. So we must know the three principal aspects of the path — renunciation, Bodhichitta, and right view — in order to practise Tantra, and then think and shape our mind properly. Then the practise of Tantra becomes the union of Sutra and Tantra. The life force on any path, whether it be Sutra or Tantra, is precious Bodhichitta. Therefore, it is extremely important.

How can we judge, on the basis of the word of the Buddha, which philosophies are more advanced and profound, when each sutra teaches that the doctrine it proclaims is supreme? Which can be held as true? If we trust one sutra, how can we regard others that contradict it? If we have to prove that one sutra is true and that another is false by relying on another word of the Buddha, the process becomes infinite. Therefore, the differentiation of schools that are advanced must be on the basis of reasoning. The Mahayana Sutras tell us that we must divide the teachings of the Buddha into those which need to be interpreted and those which can be taken literally. Buddha said:

> *Bhikshus and wise men,*
> *As one essays gold by rubbing, cutting and melting,*
> *So examine well my words,*
> *And accept them,*
> *But not because you respect me.*

The meaning of this has been clearly explained by Lord Maitreya in the Mahayana-sutra-alankara-karika by means of the four dependencies:

1. Of the teacher: depend not only on the teacher's person, but on what he teaches

2. Of the teaching: depend not merely on the sweetness of the words and so on, but on the meaning

3. Of the meaning: depend not on the interpretive meaning which must be understood in a different way, being controvertible since it was taught with a specific intent or under a specific circumstance, but depend upon the definitive meaning

4. Of the definitive meaning: depend not on a consciousness with dualistic views, but on a non-conceptual direct knowledge focused on the Deep One (shunyata)

CHAPTER 14

Compassion and Cultivating the Compassion Within

· ·

What need is there to say more?
The childish work for their own benefit,
The Buddhas work for the benefit of others,
Just look at the difference between them.

—Shantideva

Compassion for others (as opposed to self) is one of the central teachings of Mahayana Buddhism. I would like to quote a verse which conveys this message:

If you are unable to exchange your happiness
For the suffering of other beings,
You have no hope of attaining Buddhahood
Nor even of happiness in this present life.

The essence of the Mahayana school, which we try to practice, is compassion. In Mahayana Buddhism, you sacrifice yourself in order to attain salvation for the sake of other beings.

Avalokiteshwara is conceived as the Lord of Mercy, but the real Avalokiteshwara is compassion itself. This undiscriminating, unmotivated and unlimited compassion for all is obviously not the usual love that you have for your friends, relatives or family. The love which is limited to your near and dear ones is alloyed with ignorance, with attachment. The kind of love we advocate is the love you can have for someone who has done harm to you. This kind of love is to be extended to all living beings.

The rationale for loving others is the recognition of the simple fact that every living being has the same right to, and the same desire for, happiness and not suffering; and the consideration that you as one individual are one life-unit as compared with the multitude of others in their ceaseless quest for happiness. According to the Mahayana school of Buddhism, you must not only think in terms of human beings like this, but of all sentient beings. And, ultimately, all sentient beings have the potentiality to attain Buddhahood.

In our approach to life, be it pragmatic or otherwise, a basic fact that confronts us squarely and unmistakably is the desire for peace, security and happiness. Different forms of life at different levels of existence make up the teeming denizens of this earth of ours. And no matter whether they belong to the higher groups such as human beings, or to the lower groups such as animals, all beings primarily seek peace, comfort and security. Life is as dear to a mute creature as it is to a man. Even the lowliest insect strives for protection from dangers that threaten its life. Just as each one of us wants happiness and fears pain, just as each one of us wants to live and not to die, so do all the other creatures.

The faculty of reasoning, the ability to think and the power of expression distinguish man as a being superior to his mute friends. In the quest for peace, comfort and security, the methods used by man are diverse and, sometimes, radically opposed to one another. All too frequently, the means adopted are cruel and revolting.

Behaving in a way that is utterly unbecoming to his human status, man indulges in inhuman cruelties, torturing his fellow men as well as members of the animal kingdom, just for the sake of selfish gain; such behaviour has almost become the order of the day. Such unskilled actions bring suffering to oneself as well as to others. Having been born as human beings, it is vitally important for us to practice benevolence and perform meritorious deeds for ourselves and others in this life and in lives to come. To be born a human being is a rare experience, and it is wise to use this golden opportunity as effectively and skilfully as possible.

Buddhism, with its emphasis on universal love and compassion, impregnated with ideas that are wholly non-violent and peaceful, offers a means, at once unique and eternal, for the successful attainment of that state of security and happiness from where man and beast can derive common benefit. It can be asserted rightly that loving-kindness and compassion are the two cornerstones on which the whole edifice of Buddhism stands. Destruction or injury to life is strictly forbidden. Harming or destroying any being from the highest to the lowest, from the human to the tiniest insect must be avoided at all costs.

The Blessed One said: "Do not harm others. Just as you feel affection on seeing a dearly beloved person, so should you extend loving-kindness to all creatures." Those who follow the way of Mahayana are admonished not only to abstain from injuring, but also to cultivate a great spirit of compassion, with an eager longing to save all sentient beings from pain and misery.

The arising of Mahakaruna in the mind will prepare the ground for the perfect fruition of the precious Bodhimind, which is a necessary condition for attaining the supreme status of a Bodhisattva. One is called a Bodhisattva when one's mind is filled with the pure compassion and equanimity which proceed from Bodhimind. As whatever we do in our everyday life arises from the functioning of our minds, ultimate peace and Buddhahood are the result of Bodhimind and compassion. The Lord Buddha has said: "Bodhimind is the seed of all dharmas." The intention to do good to others, the persistent thought in one's heart of the welfare of others, will create happiness among the people around us. To return good for evil, benevolence for injury, love for hate, and compassion for harm, are some of the characteristics of the qualities of Bodhimind. Deeds of benevolence and loving-kindness, not responding to ill-will from others, will delight the hearts of all. Indulgence in resentment and vengeance will only further and increase miseries to oneself and others in this life and in lives to come.

Whatever method is adopted for the cultivation of the quality of Bodhimind, the fact remains that the birth-cycles of all sentient beings are beginningless, and that numberless times in their previous lives they have each fulfilled the role of a mother. The feeling of a mother for her child is a classic example of love. For the safety, protection and welfare of her children, a mother is ready to sacrifice her very life. Recognising this, children should be grateful to their mothers and express their gratitude by performing virtuous deeds. In the same way, a person motivated by the thought of Bodhimind strives with all his might for the welfare of every sentient being, whether it is a human or a beast or a fowl, of land or sea. At the same time, he will treat all beings as he treats his mother. In repayment of her maternal love, it will be his constant endeavour to do only that which is benevolent. Thus, cultivation of compassion and loving-kindness for all sentient beings brings peace and happiness to oneself and others. Ill-will, malice and malevolent acts will only be a source of suffering to all.

The noble aspiration to attain Buddhahood, to cultivate Bodhimind in thought and to practise charity, forbearance, morality, kindness, and so on, are all for the sake of living beings. It is for them that these ennobling and uplifting qualities are sought. The creatures that inhabit this earth — be they be human beings or animals — are here to contribute, each in its own peculiar way, to the beauty and prosperity of the world. Many creatures have toiled singly or jointly to make our life comfortable. The food we eat, the clothes we wear, have not just dropped from the sky. Many creatures have laboured to produce them. That is why we should be grateful to all our fellow creatures. Compassion and loving-kindness are the hallmarks of achievement and happiness. Let us practise them for the welfare of all.

We must realise that human happiness is interdependent. One's own successful or happy future is related to that of others. Therefore, helping others and being considerate and sensitive to their rights and needs is actually not only one's responsibility, but a matter of one's own happiness. So, I often tell people, if we have to be really selfish, then let us be wisely selfish. If we are warm-hearted, we automatically receive more smiles and make more genuine friends. We human beings are social animals. No matter how powerful or how intelligent we are, it is virtually impossible to survive without other human beings. We need others for our very existence. The practice of compassion and non-violence is therefore in one's own self interest.

Genuine non-violence is related to one's mental attitude. When we talk of peace, we must mean genuine peace, not merely the absence of war. For example, in the last few decades there was relative peace on the European continent, but I do not think it was genuine peace. It was peace that came out of fear as a result of the Cold War.

What is the relevance of non-violence and compassion in today's world? Ahimsa, or non-violence, is an ancient

Indian concept, which Mahatma Gandhi revived and implemented in modern times — not only in politics, but also in day-to-day life. This was his great achievement. The nature of non-violence should be something that is not passive, but active in helping others. Non-violence means that, if you can help and serve others, you must. If you cannot, you must at least restrain yourself from harming others.

The twentieth century, I think, is the most important century in human history. It has seen many outstanding scientific achievements and, yet, more human suffering than ever before. The human being in this century is basically the same as a thousand or ten thousand years ago. He has had the [same] negative feelings of anger and hatred; but this century has seen an enormous increase in his destructive power. This has produced a desperate situation of fear. With the possibility of the nuclear holocaust, the picture seems hopeless and unbearable. The future looks so bleak, that it has forced, and helped, the human mind to think of alternatives. This gives us great hope.

During the fifties and sixties, many people felt that the ultimate decision in any disagreement or conflict could only come through war, or weapons that were believed to deter war. Today, more and more people are realising that the proper way of resolving differences is through dialogue, compromise, negotiations — through human understanding and humility. It is a very good sign.

The events and developments of our country have encouraged the human being to become wiser, more mature. In many countries, I think the attraction to Gandhian philosophy is growing. Because the capacity for human destruction is so immense, because the threat to the environment is so great, people are developing a greater understanding of the meaning of non-violence and compassion.

Sometimes, people feel that human beings are not all that gentle; after all there is so much violence, so much killing, so much tragedy. But, if you look closely, of the more than five billion human beings, the number who are engaging in negative activities or have negative thoughts is very small. If human nature was so bad, I think, we would not have had to worry about the population problem.

Compassion and love are not matters of religion, though many religions teach these things. When we are born, we do not have any religion, but we are not without human love and affection. This is not a matter of religion. I believe it is a separate thing. What religions do is try to strengthen these qualities, which are already there in human nature from birth.

Why is it necessary to make a distinction between religion and human nature? This is essential because, of the five billion or so people on our planet, not more than about one billion are believers, or directly follow any organised religion. We are all members of the same human family. We must find ways of cultivating a deeper awareness of love and compassion, with or without religion. At the same time, we need to understand the negative expressions of the human mind — such as anger, hatred and attachment.

What is anger? It is true that, sometimes, due to some tragedy in our lives or due to frustrated desires, we feel negative feelings which express themselves more openly in anger. This may sometimes seem useful. But we must analyse and investigate the value of anger. Anger brings forth extra energy, boldness and determination. It is possible to use this energy to take certain drastic actions. Usually, decisions taken when your mind is dominated by anger are wrong decisions, which bring unhappiness or regret. When we face some external problem, it is often possible to escape it and find a solution, but when the anger or hatred is within, you cannot do so easily. Once you have an understanding or realisation of the nature of your mind, then gradually it will change. As time goes on your attitude, even to the external enemy, will change. With understanding, there will be forgiveness and an increase of your inner strength. As a result, there will be less fear, less doubt and more self confidence, tolerance and patience. This is why I consider compassion to be the key.

We are human beings; our basic nature is that of love and compassion. When we see a tree with some branches dying, we are sad. When we see greenery and buds growing into flowers we feel positive and happy. In human nature, there is a natural feeling for living things. I think the time has come to think about the basic cause of our suffering.

CHAPTER 15

Altruism: Cherishing Others

●●●●●●●●●●●●●●●●●●●●●●●●●

All the pain that exists in the world,
All the terror and misery to be found,
Originates from the self-cherishing attitude,
What other ghost needs to be exorcised?

— Old scripture

The main theme of Buddhism is altruism based on compassion and love. The feeling of compassion is important whether you are a believer or non-believer, for everyone shares or feels the value of love. When we human beings are small children, we depend very much on the kindness of our parents; without their kindness, it would be difficult to survive. Again, when we become very old, we need the kindness of others — we are dependent on it. Between the two — childhood and old age — we are quite independent, feeling that, since we have no need to depend on others, we ourselves do not need to practise kindness. This is wrong.

In order to have genuine consideration for others' happiness and welfare, it is necessary to have a special altruistic attitude, in which you take upon yourself the burden of helping others. In order to generate such an unusual attitude, it is necessary to have great compassion, to care about the suffering of others and to want to do something about it. In order to have such a strong force of compassion, you must first have a strong sense of love which, upon observing suffering sentient beings, wishes that they had happiness — finding a pleasantness in everyone, and wishing happiness for everyone, just as a mother does for her only, sweet child.

Again, in order to have a sense of closeness and dearness regarding others, you must first train in a sense of kindness, through using as a model a person in this lifetime who was very kind to you and then extending this sense of gratitude to all beings. Since, in general, in this life your mother was probably the closest and offered the most help, the process of meditation begins with recognising the fact that all other sentient beings are like your mother.

This system of meditation has seven steps:

1. Recognising all sentient beings as mothers

2. Becoming mindful of their kindness

3. Developing an intention to repay their kindness

4. Love

5. Compassion

6. The unusual attitude

7. The altruistic intention to become enlightened

If you consider the matter in depth and in detail, even great enemies who, for a period of time, single-pointedly harmed you, actually extended great kindness to you. The reason is this: from an enemy you can learn tolerance and patience, whereas from a religious teacher or your parents, the strength of your tolerance cannot be tested. Only when faced with enemies, can you develop real inner strength.

From this viewpoint, even enemies are teachers of inner strength, courage and determination. Because you have an enemy, you may also come closer to reality, peeling off pretensions. After you become mindful of others' kindness, you feel like repaying it. How is it to be repaid?

The next step is to generate a sense of love, wishing for the happiness of all sentient beings, wishing that beings bereft of happiness have happiness and all of its causes. As much as you view sentient beings with love, finding a sense of pleasantness in everyone and cherishing them, so much do you generate the next step, compassion — a wish that they are freed from suffering and all of its causes.

The generation of love and compassion involves a change of attitude on your part, but the beings who are the objects of these feelings are still suffering. So, having generated love and compassion, the next step is to extend these altruistic attitudes beyond just the thought, "How nice it would be if they were free from suffering and its causes and came to possess happiness and its causes," and develop the stronger thought, "I will cause them to be free from suffering and its causes and to be endowed with happiness and its causes."

Here, you develop the strong determination, not just to generate such good attitudes in the mind, but actually free those beings from suffering and establish them in happiness through your own effort. This laudable intention will endow you with great courage to take on the great burden of the welfare of all sentient beings. When you have this strength of mind, as great as the hardships are, so great will be your sense of determination and courage. Hardship will assist your determination.

Practising altruism is the real source of cooperation; merely recognising our need for harmony is not enough. A mind committed to compassion is like an overflowing reservoir — a constant source of energy, determination and kindness. This mind is like a seed; when cultivated, it gives rise to many other good qualities, such as forgiveness, tolerance, inner strength and the confidence to overcome fear and insecurity. The compassionate mind is like an elixir; it is capable of transforming bad situations into beneficial ones. Therefore, we should not limit our expression of love and compassion to our family and friends. Nor is compassion only the responsibility of the clergy, health-care and social workers. It is the necessary business of every member of the human community.

A self-cherishing attitude is like a chronic disease. We become like only half a person through being afflicted with this attitude, even though we have a mind and the ability to discriminate between right and wrong. So, we must put effort into eliminating this chronic disease. The mind which cherishes others more than self is the source of every imaginable benefit. It can be compared to holy medicine which cures disease, or to a precious substance like nectar. It is our inner spiritual master, the supreme cause of Buddhahood and the unsurpassable remover of the suffering of sentient beings.

What is the use of our own happiness, when all mothers who have been kind to us since beginningless time are suffering ?

Therefore, it is the practice of the Bodhisattva to generate Bodhichitta in order to liberate all sentient beings.

CHAPTER 16

The Six Perfections

• •

From the Buddhist viewpoint, what kind of help can we give others? One important type of charity is the giving of material things such as food, clothing and shelter to others, but it is limited, for it does not bring complete satisfaction. Our own experience confirms that, through gradual purification of our own mind, more and more happiness develops; it is the same for others. Thus, it is crucial that they understand what they should adopt in practice in order to achieve happiness. To facilitate their learning these topics, we need to be fully capable of teaching them. Moreover, since sentient beings have limitlessly different predispositions, interests, dormant potentialities and attitudes, if we do not develop the exalted activities of speech that accord exactly with what other beings need, we cannot fulfil all their hopes. There is no way to accomplish this, unless we overcome the obstructions preventing omniscience in our own mental continuums. Thus, out of seeking to help others, we come to a decision to attain the stage of Buddhahood, in which the obstructions to omniscience have been extinguished.

In this way, the Bodhisattva attitude is described as the attitude of a mind aiming for the welfare of others as its special object of intent, and also aspiring towards its own Buddhahood in order to accomplish it. Though your final aim is altruistic service upon the attainment of Buddhahood, in terms of actual implementation in the present moment, you engage in the practice of the six perfections—giving, ethics, patience, effort, concentration and wisdom — in accordance with your capacity, beginning with the charity of giving material things.

Charity means to train from the depths of the heart in an attitude of generosity such that you are not seeking any reward or result for yourself. From the depths of your heart, the act of charity, and all of its beneficial results, are dedicated to other sentient beings.

Concerning ethics, the root practice of a Bodhisattva is to restrain self-centredness. Since the practice of charity cannot involve any harm to others if it is to succeed, it is necessary to pull out any tendency to harm others from the very root. This must be done through eliminating self-centredness, since a wholly altruistic attitude leaves no room for harming others. Thus, the ethic of restraining self centredness is crucial.

In order to attain purity in ethics, it is necessary to cultivate patience. The practice of patience is extremely important, since it is the main bulwark and prepares the ground for training in the equalising and switching of self and others. It is most helpful to practise it in tandem with the techniques that Shantideva sets forth in the chapters on patience and on concentration in the *Guide to a Bodhisattva's Way of Life;* in the latter, he explains the equalising and switching of self and others. The practice of patience establishes the foundation, the basis, for equalising and switching self and others. The reason for this is that it is hardest to generate a sense of affection and respect for enemies. When you think of enemies in terms of the practise of patience, not only is an enemy not someone who harms you, an enemy is the most benevolent of helpers. You come to think, "There would be no way I could cultivate the patience of not being concerned about harm to myself without someone to harm me."

As Shantideva says, there are many beings who give one an opportunity to practise charity, but there are very few beings with respect to whom one can practise patience, and what is more rare is more valuable. An enemy is really most kind. For this reason, enemies are the main instigators of the increase of meritorious power. An enemy is not someone who prevents the practice of religion but someone who helps practice.

The fourth of the six perfections is effort. One type of effort is like putting on armour; it prevents dissatisfaction with the lack of immediate achievement. Effort circumscribes a willingness to engage in enthusiastic practice for eons and eons in order to increase our merit; and patience can only be practised in dependence upon development.

When you have made such an effort, you have the necessary prerequisites for developing concentration. Concentration is a matter of channelising this mind, which is presently distracted, and pulled in a great many directions. A scattered mind, does not have much power. When channelised, no matter what the object of observation is, the mind is very powerful. There is no external way to channelise the mind, as by a surgical operation; it must be done by withdrawing it within. Withdrawal of the mind also occurs in deep sleep, in which the factor of alertness has become unclear; therefore, here, the withdrawal of the mind is to be accompanied by the very strong clarity of alertness. In brief, the mind must have the stability, staying firmly focused on its object, with great clarity of the object, an alert, clear, sharp tautness.

With respect to the last perfection, wisdom, in general, there are many types of wisdom. The three main ones are: conventional wisdom realising the five fields of knowledge; ultimate wisdom realising the mode of subsistence of phenomena; and wisdom knowing how to help sentient beings.

CHAPTER 17

Oneself and Others: Exchanging Places

• •

If I do not exchange my happiness
For the suffering of others,
I shall not attain the state of Buddhahood
And even in samsara I shall have no real joy.
—Shantideva

Equalising oneself and others means to develop the attitude and understanding of, "Just as I desire happiness and wish to avoid suffering, the same is true of all other living beings, who are infinite as space; they too desire happiness and wish to avoid suffering." Shantideva explains that, just as we work for our own benefit in order to gain happiness and protect ourselves from suffering, we should also work for the benefit of others, to help them attain happiness and freedom from suffering.

Shantideva argues that, although there are different parts of our body — such as our head, limbs, and so on — insofar as the need to protect them is concerned, there is no difference amongst them, for they are all equally parts of the same body. In the same manner, all sentient beings have this natural tendency — wishing to attain happiness and be free from suffering — and, insofar as that natural inclination is concerned, there is no difference whatsoever between all sentient beings. Consequently, we should not discriminate between ourselves and others in working to gain happiness and overcome suffering.

We should reflect upon and make serious efforts to dissolve our present attitude, that views ourselves and others as being separate and distinct. We have seen that, insofar as the wish to gain happiness and to avoid suffering is concerned, there is no difference at all. The same is also true of our natural right to be happy; just as we have the right to enjoy happiness and freedom from suffering, all other living beings have the same natural right. So where is the difference? The difference lies in the number of sentient beings involved. When we speak of our welfare, we are speaking of the welfare of only one individual, whereas the welfare of others encompasses the well being of an infinite number of beings. From that point of view, we understand that others' welfare is much more important than our own.

If our own and others' welfare were totally unrelated and independent of each other, we could make a case for neglecting others' welfare. But that is not the case. I am always related to others and heavily dependent on them: while I am an ordinary person, while I am on the path, and also once I have achieved the resultant state. If we reflect along these lines, the importance of working for the benefit of others emerges naturally.

We should also examine whether, by remaining selfish and self-centred despite the validity of the above points, we can still achieve happiness and fulfill our desires. If that were the case, the pursuit of our selfish and self-centred habits would be a reasonable course of action. But it is not. The nature of our existence is such that we must depend on the cooperation and kindness of others for our survival. It is an observable fact that, the more we take the welfare of others to heart and work for their benefit, the more benefit we attain for ourselves. On the other hand, the more selfish and self centred we remain, the more lonely and miserable we become.

Therefore, if we definitely want to work for our own benefit and welfare then, as the Bodhicaryavatara recommends, it is better to take into account the welfare of others and to regard their welfare as more important than our own.

Let me describe how this is practised in meditation. This is my own practice, and I frequently speak about it to others. Imagine that in front of you, on one side, is your old selfish 'I' and that, on the other side, is a group of poor, needy people. And you yourself are in the middle as a neutral person, a third party. Then judge which is more important — whether you should join this selfish, self centred, stupid person or these poor needy, helpless people. If you have a human heart, naturally you will be drawn to the side of the needy beings. This type of reflective contemplation will help in developing an altruistic attitude. The ultimate source of peace in the family, the country and the world is altruism — compassion and love. Contemplation of this fact also helps us tremendously as we try to develop altruism.

All religions — in teaching moral precepts to mould the functions of mind, body and speech — primarily have the same noble goal. They all teach us not to lie or bear false witness, not to steal or take others' lives, and so on. That there are so many different religions to bring happiness to mankind is analogous to the treatment of a particular disease by different methods. For, in the most general terms, all religions aim to help each living being avoid misery and acquire happiness. Thus, although we can find causes for preferring individual interpretations of religious truth, there is much greater cause for unity stemming from the heart. In the present state of the world, the need to evolve a great measure of unity among the followers of different religions has become especially important. Moreover, such unity is not an impossible ideal.

Bodhimind forms the central theme of Mahayana Buddhism in Tibet. The Blessed One acquired Bodhimind after making innumerable sacrifices and powerfully concentrated efforts. For three immeasurable eons, he practised the deeds of a Bodhisattva, making unstinting sacrifices and undergoing great hardships, thus gradually acquiring the dual accumulations of merit and wisdom.

The inspiration to achieve this ineffable Bodhimind can be expressed in this way: "I must attain the supreme state of omniscient Buddhahood, so that I can liberate all sentient beings."

CHAPTER 18

Recognising the Enemy Within

• • • • • • • • • • • • • • • • • •

The greatest obstacle to cultivating compassion and a good heart is selfishness: the attitude of cherishing one's own welfare and benefit, often remaining oblivious to the well being of others. This self-centred attitude underlies most of our ordinary states of mind, as well as the various states of existence in samsara, and is thus the root of all delusions. Therefore, the first task of a practitioner of compassion and a good heart is to gain an understanding of the destructive nature of these delusions, and how they naturally lead to undesirable consequences.

In the fourth chapter of Bodhicaryavatara, entitled *Consciousness,* Shantideva explains that delusions such as hatred, anger, attachment and jealousy, which reside within our minds, are our true enemies. As can be seen from the following two verses:

> *Enemies such as hatred and craving*
> *Have neither arms nor legs,*
> *And are neither courageous nor wise;*
> *How, then, have I been used like a slave by them?*

> *For, while they dwell within my mind,*
> *At their pleasure they cause me harm;*
> *Yet I patiently endure them without anger*
> *But this is an inappropriate and shameful time for*
> *patience.*

Negative thoughts and emotions are often deceptive. They play tricks on us. Desire, for example, appears to us as a trusted friend, something beautiful and dear to us. Similarly, anger and hatred appear to us like our protectors or reliable bodyguards. Sometimes, when someone is about to harm us, anger rises up like a protector and gives us a kind of strength. Even though we may be physically weaker than our assailants, anger makes us feel strong. It gives us a false sense of power and energy, the result being, in this case, that we might get beaten up. Because anger and other destructive emotions appear in such deceptive ways, we never actually challenge them. In order to fully realise the treachery of these negative thoughts and emotions, we must first achieve a calm state of mind. Only then will we begin to see their treacherous nature.

One of the best human qualities is intelligence, which enables us to judge what is wholesome, and what is unwholesome and what is harmful. Negative thoughts, such as anger and strong attachment, destroy this special human quality; this is indeed very sad.

When anger or attachment dominates the mind, a person becomes almost crazed, and I am certain that nobody wishes to be crazy. Under their power, we commit all kinds of acts — often with far-reaching and destructive consequences. A person gripped by such states of mind and emotions is like a blind person, who cannot see where he is going. Yet, we fail to challenge these negative thoughts and emotions, which lead to near insanity. On the contrary, we often nurture and reinforce them. By doing so we are, in fact, allowing ourselves to fall prey to their destructive power. When we reflect along these lines, we will realise that our true enemy is not outside ourselves.

Usually, we define our enemy as a person, an external agent, whom we believe is causing harm to us or to someone we hold dear. But such an enemy is relative and impermanent. One moment, the person may act as an enemy; at yet another moment, he or she may become your best friend. This is a truth that we often experience in our own lives. But negative thoughts and emotions, the inner enemy, will always remain the enemy. They are our enemies today, they have been our enemies in the past, and they will remain our enemies in the future — as long as they reside within our mental continuums. Therefore, Shantideva says that negative thoughts and emotions are the real enemy, and this enemy is within. This inner enemy is extremely dangerous. The destructive potential of an external enemy is limited, compared to that of his inner counterpart. The only effective means of overcoming the inner enemy is through gaining a deep insight into the mind, and clearly realising its nature.

Despite its pervasive influence and destructive potential, there is one particular way in which the inner enemy is weaker than the external enemy. Shantideva explains in the *Bodhicaryavatara* that, to overcome ordinary enemies, you need physical strength. But to combat the enemy within, the disturbing conceptions, you need only develop the factors that give rise to the wisdom realising the ultimate nature of phenomena. You must also genuinely understand both the relative nature of negative thoughts and emotions, as well as the ultimate nature of all phenomena. In technical Buddhist terminology, this insight is known as the true insight into the nature of emptiness. Shantideva mentions still another sense in which the inner enemy is weaker. Unlike an external enemy, the inner enemy cannot regroup and launch a comeback, once he has been destroyed from within.

CHAPTER 19

Dealing with
Anger and Hatred
• •

Hatred and anger are the greatest obstacles for a practitioner of Bodhichitta. Bodhisattvas should never generate hatred; instead, they should counteract it. To achieve this, the practice of patience, or tolerance, is crucial. Shantideva begins the sixth chapter of his text, entitled *Patience*, by explaining the seriousness of the harm and damage caused by anger and hatred: they harm us now and in the future, and they also harm us by destroying our collection of past merits. Since the practitioner of patience must counteract and overcome hatred, Shantideva emphasises the importance of first identifying the factors that cause anger and hatred. The principal cause is dissatisfaction and unhappiness. When we are unhappy and dissatisfied, we easily become frustrated and this leads to feelings of hatred and anger.

Shantideva explains that it is very important for those of us training in patience to prevent mental unhappiness from arising — as is prone to occur when you feel that you or your loved ones are threatened, when misfortune befalls you or when others obstruct you from reaching your goals. Your feelings of dissatisfaction and unhappiness on these occasions fuel your hatred and anger. So right from the beginning, it is important not to allow such circumstances to disturb your peace of mind. He emphasises that we should, with all the means at our disposal, counteract and eliminate the onset of hatred, since its only function is to harm us and others. This is very profound advice.

If maintaining a balanced and happy state of mind even in the face of adversity is a key factor in preventing hatred from arising, we may still wonder how to achieve it. Shantideva says that when you are faced with adverse circumstances, feeling unhappy serves no purpose in overcoming the undesirable situation. It is not only futile but will, in fact, only serve to aggravate your own anxiety and bring about an uncomfortable and dissatisfied state of mind. You will lose all sense of composure and happiness. Anxiety and unhappiness gradually eat away at your insides and affect your sleep patterns, your appetite and your health. In fact, if the initial harm you experienced was inflicted by an enemy, your mental unhappiness may even become a source of delight for that person. Therefore, it is pointless to feel unhappy and dissatisfied when faced with adverse circumstances or, for that matter, to retaliate against those who caused you harm.

Shantideva further reasons that, if the problem can be resolved, there is no need to be overly concerned or disturbed. On the other hand, if nothing can be done to resolve the difficulty, it is useless to feel unhappy about it. Either way, being unhappy and overwhelmed by the difficulty is not an appropriate response.

Generally, there are two types of hatred or anger that result from unhappiness and dissatisfaction. One type is when someone inflicts harm upon you; and, as a result, you feel unhappy and generate anger. Another type is when, although no person may be directly inflicting harm upon you, as a result of seeing the success and prosperity of your enemies, you feel unhappy and generate anger on that basis.

Similarly, there are two types of harm caused by others. One type is direct physical harm inflicted by others and consciously experienced by you. The other type is the harming of your material possessions, reputation, friendship, and so on. Though not directed at your body, these acts also harm you in a way.

When you feel angry with others who are not causing you direct physical harm, but whom you perceive as getting in the way of your acquisition of fame, position, material gains, and so on, you should think in the following manner: "Why should I get especially upset or angry about this particular problem?" Analyse the nature of what you are being kept from obtaining — fame and so on — and examine carefully how it benefits you. Are they really that important? You will find that they are not. Since that is the case, why be so angry with that person? Thinking this way is also useful.

When you get angry as a result of the unhappiness you feel at seeing your enemy's success and prosperity, you should remember that simply being hateful, angry or unhappy, is not going to affect that person's material possessions or success in life. Therefore, even from that point of view, it is quite pointless.

If we investigate at a still deeper level, we will find that, when enemies inflict harm on us, we can actually feel gratitude towards them. Such situations provide us with a rare opportunity to test our own practice of patience. It is a precious occasion to practise not only patience, but the other Bodhisattva ideals as well. As a result, we have the opportunity to accumulate merit in these situations and to receive the benefits thereof. The poor enemy, on the other hand, because of the negative action of inflicting harm on someone out of anger and hatred, must eventually face the consequences of his or her own actions. It is almost as if the perpetrator of the harm sacrifices himself or herself for the sake of our benefit. Since the merit accumulated from the practice of patience was possible only because of the opportunity provided us by our enemy, strictly speaking, we should dedicate our merit to the benefit of that enemy. This is why the Bodhicaryavatara speaks of the kindness of the enemy.

Shantideva concludes the chapter on *Patience* by explaining the benefits of practising patience. To summarise through practicing patience, you will not only reach a state of omniscience in the future but, even in your everyday life, you will experience its practical benefits. You will be able to maintain your peace of mind and live a joyful life. When you practice patience to overcome hatred and anger, it is important to be equipped with the force of joyous effort. We should be skilful in cultivating joyous effort. Shantideva explains that, just as we must be mindful when undertaking an ordinary task such as waging war, to inflict the greatest possible destruction on the enemy while protecting ourselves from the enemy's harm, in the same way, when we undertake the practice of joyous effort, it is important to attain the greatest level of success, while assuring that this action does not damage or hinder our other practices.

CHAPTER 20

Consciousness and the 'I'

•••••••••••••••••••••••••••••••••

There are many different ways in which the 'I' appears. One is for the 'I' to appear to be factually different from the aggregates of mind and body and to be permanent, unitary and under its own power. Another is for the 'I' within not appearing to be factually other than the aggregates, to appear to be the bearer of the burden of the aggregates, or the master of a substantially existent or self-sufficient 'I'. Another way is for the 'I' to appear to be not posited through appearing to an awareness, but to be established from the side of its own uncommon mode of subsistence. Another is for the 'I' to appear to be inherently existent in its own right, not seeming to exist through the force of nominality. There is also another way in which, even though the 'I' appears to exist in its own right, a mere 'I' is all that is conceived. The conception of this last one is the only valid cognition among these.

What is the 'I' ? When it is sought analytically, it cannot be found. Nothing among the mental and physical aggregates, nor the continuum of them, nor their collection can be posited as something that is the 'I'. When a speckled coil of rope in the dark appears to you to be a snake due to the darkness of its location, the parts of the rope together, the continuum of those parts over time — none of these can be posited as a snake. The snake exists only through the force of the mind of the fearful person; from the existential reality of the rope there is nothing that is established as a snake.

As in that example, nothing among the mental and physical aggregates which are the basis of designation of the 'I', either separately or together or as their continuum over time, can be posited as something that is the 'I'. Also, it is completely impossible to find the 'I' as a factuality separate from the mind and body, which are the basis of designation of the 'I'. Now, if you began to think that therefore the 'I' does not exist at all, this would be contradicted by conventional valid cognition. The fact that the 'I' exists is obvious.

The existence of the 'I' is certified by experience, by valid cognition, but it is undiscountable among its bases of designation. Thus, the 'I' only exists in a designated manner, through the force of nominality or conceptuality, through a subjective force. On what does it nominally depend? Its mere nominal existence is posited in dependence upon its basis of designation.

With regard to the mental and physical aggregates which are its basis of designation, and among which there are many grosser and subtler levels, the subtlest is the beginningless consciousness that goes throughout all lifetimes. Therefore, it is said that 'I' is designated through the power of nominality in dependence upon this continuum of consciousness. The conclusion is that, except for a self that exists through the power of nominality, there is no self that is established from its own viewpoint. This lack of establishment of the object in its own right is the meaning of selflessness.

You might ask, "If the 'I' and so on exist through the power of conceptuality, are these designates mine or yours, in the past, present or whatever?" This is again a case of analysing to try to find the object designated, and you will not find it as such. The Buddha said that all phenomena are only nominal and that mere nominality itself is only nominal. Emptiness itself is empty. Even the Buddha is empty of inherent existence. Through emptiness, the extreme of the ramification of existence is avoided, but through the fact that things are not utterly non-existent, the extreme of utter non-existence is avoided.

CHAPTER 21

Selflessness

• • • • • • • • • • • • •

I t is necessary to know what self is—to identify the self
that does not exist. Only then can one understand its
opposite, selflessness. Selflessness is not a case of something
that existed in the past becoming non-existent; rather, this
sort of self is something that never existed. What is needed
is to identify as non-existent something that always was
non-existent; because, due to not having made such an
identification, we are drawn into the afflictive emotions of
desire and hatred, as well as all the problems these bring.

What is this self that does not exist? In this context, self
refers not to the person or 'I' as it usually does, but to
independence, something that exists under its own power.
You should examine all types of phenomena to determine
if they exist under their own power, to see whether they
have their own independent mode of subsistence or not.
If phenomena do exist under their own power, then when
you investigate to find the object designated, it should
become clearer and clearer.

For instance, consider your own person (the usual type
of self) or 'I'. The 'I' appears from within the context of
mind and body; however, if you investigate and examine
these places from which it appears, you cannot find it.
Similarly, with regard to this table, if you are not satisfied
with its mere appearance, but investigate its nature,
searching for its various parts and separating all of its

qualities and so on, there is no table left to be found as the substrate of those parts and qualities.

The fact that things cannot be found as a result of analysis when you search to find the object designated, indicates that phenomena do not exist under their own power. Objects are not established objectively in and of themselves, but do indeed exist; even if, through a primary analysis, I search to find the table and cannot find it, if I hit it with my fist, it will hurt my knuckles. Thus, its existence is indicated by my own experience. However, the fact that it cannot be found under analysis indicates that it does not exist in its own right, objectively, and thus, since it exists, it is said to exist through the power of a subjective conventional consciousness.

To say that objects exist in dependence upon a subjective designating consciousness is the same as saying that they are only nominally existent. Therefore, with respect to my 'I', or person, when I search to find it among its bases of designation, mind and body, it cannot be found, and thus there is just the mere 'I' that exists through the force of conceptuality. How things appear and how they actually exist differ greatly. A person engaging in the practice of the perfection of wisdom comes out of this kind of analysis and then examines how things appear in ordinary experience, alternating analysis and comparison with the usual mode of appearance, in order to notice the discrepancy between the actual mode of subsistence of phenomena, and their appearance.

In this way, inherent existence, which is the object of negation, will become clearer and clearer. As much as the object of negation becomes clearer, so much deeper will be your understanding of emptiness. Finally, you will ascertain a mere vacuity, which is a negative of inherent existence.

Since emptiness, choosing between positive and negative phenomena, is a negative phenomenon; and, choosing between affirming negatives, and non-affirming negatives, is a non-affirming negative. When it appears to the mind, nothing will appear except an absence of such inherent existence — a mere elimination of the object of negation. Thus, for the mind of a person realising emptiness, there is no sense of, "I am ascertaining emptiness," and there is no thought, "This is emptiness." If we had such a sense, emptiness would become distant. Nevertheless, the emptiness of inherent existence is ascertained and realised.

After such realisation, even though whatever phenomena appear, appear to exist in their own right, you understand that they do not exist that way. You have a sense of their being like a magician's illusion, in that there is a combination of their appearing one way but actually existing another way. Though they appear to exist inherently, you understand that they are empty of inherent existence.

When phenomena are seen this way, the conceptions which superimpose a sense of goodness or badness on phenomena beyond what is actually there, and serve as a basis for generating desire and hatred, lessen; this is because they are based on the misconception that phenomena are established in their own right. On the other hand, those consciousnesses which have a valid foundation increase in strength. The reason for this is that the meaning of emptiness is the meaning of dependent arising. Since phenomena are dependent arisings, they are capable of increase and decrease in dependence upon conditions.

In this way, cause and effect are feasible, positable, and once cause and effect are validly positable, it can be posited that bad effects, such as suffering, can be avoided by abandoning bad causes and that good effects, such as happiness, can be achieved by embracing good causes. If phenomena did exist in their own right, they would not depend on others; and if they did not depend on others, cause and effect would be impossible. Thus, once dependence is feasible, cause and effect can be posited, and if dependence were not feasible, causes and effects could not exist.

The final reasoning that proves that things are empty of inherent existence is this very dependence on causes and conditions. When people do not understand this doctrine well, they mistakenly think that, because phenomena are empty, there is no good and bad, no cause and effect. This is a complete misunderstanding.

Knowledge of the final mode of subsistence of phenomena must be within the context of not losing the cause and effect of actions conventionally. If someone thought that, because phenomena are empty, there could not be any good or bad, even if that person repeated the word emptiness a thousand times, he or she would be moving farther and farther away from the meaning of emptiness. Hence, a person who has great interest in emptiness should pay great heed to the cause and effect of actions.

CHAPTER 22

The Concept of Mind

• •

No words can describe it
No example can point to it
Samsara does not make it worse
Nirvana does not make it better
It has never been born
It has never ceased
It has never been liberated
It has never been deluded
It has never existed
It has never been non-existent
It has no limits at all
It does not fall into any kind of category.

—Dudjom Rinpoche

One of the fundamental views in Buddhism is the principle of dependent origination. This states that all phenomena, both subjective experiences and external objects, come into existence upon causes and conditions; nothing comes into existence uncaused. Given this principle, it becomes crucial to understand what causality is and what type of causes there are. In Buddhist literature, two main categories of causation are mentioned: external causes in the form of physical objects and events, and internal causes such as cognitive and mental events.

The reason for an understanding of causality being so important in Buddhist thought and practice is that it relates directly to sentient beings, feeling of pain and pleasure and the other experiences that dominate their lives, which arise not only from internal mechanisms, but also from external causes and conditions. Therefore, it is crucial to understand not only the internal workings of mental and cognitive causation, but also their relationship to the external material world.

The fact that our inner experiences of pleasure and pain are in the nature of subjective mental and cognitive states is very obvious to us. But how these inner subjective events relate to external events and the material world poses a critical problem. The question of whether there is an external physical reality independent of sentient beings, consciousness and mind has been extensively discussed by Buddhist thinkers. Naturally, there are divergent views on this issue among the various philosophical schools of thought. One such school asserts that there is no external reality, not even external objects, and that the material world we perceive is in essence merely a projection of our minds. From many points of view, this conclusion is rather extreme. Philosophically, and for that matter conceptually, it seems more coherent to maintain a position that accepts the reality not only of the subjective world of the mind, but also of the external objects of the physical world.

Now, if we examine the origins of our inner experiences and of external matter, we find that there is a fundamental uniformity in the nature of their existence, in that both are governed by the principle of causality. Just as, in the inner world of mental and cognitive events, every moment of experience comes from its preceding continuum, and so on ad infinitum, very similarly, in the physical world, every object and event must have a preceding continuum that serves as its cause, from which the present moment of external matter comes into existence.

In some Buddhist literature we find that, in terms of the origin of its continuum, the microscopic world of our physical reality can be traced back finally to an original state, in which all material particles are condensed into what are known as space particles. If all the physical matter of our macroscopic universe can be traced to such an original state, the question then arises as to how these particles later interact with each other and evolve into a macroscopic world that can have direct bearing on sentient beings, inner experiences of pleasure and pain. To answer this, Buddhists turn to the doctrine of karma, the invisible workings of actions and their effects, which provides an explanation on how these inanimate space particles evolve into various manifestations.

The invisible workings of actions, or karmic force (karma means actions), are intimately linked to the motivation in the human mind that gives rise to these actions. Therefore, an understanding of the nature of mind and its role is crucial to an understanding of human experience, and the relationship between mind and matter. We can see from our own experience that our state of mind plays a major role in our day-to-day experience and physical and mental well being. If a person has a calm and stable mind, this influences his or her attitude and behaviour in relation to others. In other words, if someone remains in a state of mind that is calm, tranquil and peaceful, external surroundings or conditions can cause them only limited disturbance. But it is extremely difficult for someone whose mental state is restless to be calm or joyful, even when they are surrounded by the best facilities and the best of friends. This indicates that our mental attitude is a critical factor in determining our experience of joy and happiness, and thus also our good health.

There are two reasons why it is important to understand the nature of mind. One is because there is an intimate connection between mind and karma. The other is that our state of mind plays a crucial role in our experience of happiness and suffering. If understanding the mind is very important, let us ask, "What is mind, and what is its nature?"

Buddhist literature, both Sutra and Tantra, contains extensive discussions on mind and its nature. Tantra, in particular, discusses the various levels of mind and consciousness. The Sutras do not talk much about the relationship between the various states of mind and their corresponding physiological states. Tantric literature, on the other hand, is replete with references to the various subtleties of the levels of consciousness and their relationship to such physiological states as the vital energy centres within the body, the energy channels, the energies that flow within these, and so on. The Tantras also explain how, by manipulating the various physiological factors through specific meditative yogic practices, one can effect various states of consciousness.

According to Tantra, the ultimate nature of mind is essentially pure. This pristine nature is technically called 'clear light.' The various afflictive emotions such as desire, hatred and jealousy are products of conditioning. They are not intrinsic qualities of the mind, because the mind can be cleansed of them. When this clear light nature of mind is veiled or inhibited from expressing its true essence by the conditioning of the afflictive emotions and thoughts, the person is said to be caught in the cycle of existence, samsara. But when, by applying appropriate meditative techniques and practices, the individual is able to fully experience this clear light nature of mind, free from the influence and conditioning of the afflictives states, he or she is on the way to true liberation and full enlightenment.

Hence, from the Buddhist point of view, both bondage and true freedom depend on the varying states of this clear light mind, and the resultant state that meditators try to attain through the application of various meditative techniques is one in which this ultimate nature of mind fully manifests all its positive potential, enlightenment, or Buddhahood. An understanding of this clear light mind therefore becomes crucial, in the context of spiritual endeavour.

In our day-to-day experiences, especially at the gross level, our mind is interrelated with, and dependent upon, the physiological states of the body. Just as our state of mind, be it depressed or joyful, affects our physical health, so too does our physical state affect our mind. Buddhist literature mentions specific energy centres within the body that play a crucial role in increasing or decreasing the various emotions within our mind. It is because of the intimate relationship between mind and body, and the existence of these special physiological centres within our body, that physical yoga exercises and the application of special meditative techniques aimed at training the mind, can have positive effects on health.

After becoming mindful of others' kindness, a feeling of wanting to repay that kindness arises. How is it to repaid? The next step is to generate a sense of love, wishing for the happiness of all sentient beings, wishing that beings bereft of happiness have happiness and all of its causes. As much as you view sentient beings with love, finding a sense of pleasantness in everyone and cherishing them, so much do you generate the next step, compassion, which is a wish that they be free from suffering and all of its causes.

The generation of love and compassion involves a change of attitude on your part, but the beings who are the objects of these feelings are still left suffering. So, having generated love and compassion, the next step is to extend these altruistic attitudes beyond just the thought, "How nice it would be if they were free from suffering and its causes and came to possess happiness and its causes," and develop the stronger thought, "I will cause them to be free from suffering and its causes and to be endowed with happiness and its causes." Here you develop the strong determination not just to generate such good attitudes in the mind, but actually to free those beings from suffering and establish them in happiness through your own effort.

This high intention will endow you with great courage to take on the great burden of all sentient beings' welfare. When you have this strength of mind, as great as the hardships are, so great will become your sense of determination and courage. Hardship will assist your determination.

Do not commit any non-virtuous actions,
Practise perfect virtue,
Subdue your own mind:
This is the teaching of the Buddha.

CHAPTER 23

Eight Verses for Training the Mind

• •

There are many religions that set forth precepts and advice on how to adjust one's mental attitude and all, without exception, are concerned with making the mind more peaceful, disciplined, moral and ethical. In this way, the essence of all religion is the same, even though in terms of philosophy there are many differences.

The Buddhist doctrine has many finely-developed and powerful techniques capable of advancing the mind with respect to love and compassion. A good mind, a good heart, warm feelings are the most important. If you have such a good mind, you yourself will be comfortable, and your family, mate, children, parents, neighbours, and so on, will be happy as well. Thus, in human society, goodwill and kindness are the most important things. They are very precious and necessary in one's life, and it is worthwhile to make an effort to develop a good heart.

We should take this good heart, this altruism, as the very basis and internal structure of our practice and should direct whatever virtuous activities we perform towards its increase. We should suffuse our minds with it thoroughly, and should also use words, or writings, as means of reminding ourselves of the practice. An example of such writing is the *Eight Stanzas for Training the Mind.*

The composer of this text, the Kadampa master Geshe Langri Thangpa, saw the practice of the mind of enlightenment, and in particular the meditation of exchanging self with others, as most important throughout his life.

I shall explain the eight verses briefly.

> 1. *With a determination to accomplish*
> *The highest welfare for all sentient beings,*
> *Who surpass even a wish-granting jewel*
> *I will learn to hold them supremely dear.*

Sentient beings' kindness to us is not confined to the achievement of our final goal, enlightenment. The fulfilment of our temporary aims, such as the experience of happiness, also depends upon their kindness.

Therefore, sentient beings are superior even to the wish-fulfilling jewel. So we make the prayer, "May I at all times hold them dear." We should regard them as being more precious than a wish-fulfilling jewel.

> 2. *Whenever I associate with others I will learn*
> *To think of myself as the lowest among all*
> *And respectfully hold others to be supreme*
> *From the very depths of my heart.*

When we meet others, we should not think of ourselves as superior and look down on them or pity them, but think of ourselves as more humble than they are. We should hold them dear and revere them, because they have a capacity equal to the activities of the Buddhas, to grant us happiness and enlightenment.

> 3. *In all actions I will learn to search my mind*
> *And as soon as an afflictive emotion arises*
> *Endangering myself and others*
> *Will firmly face and avert it.*

When we engage in ritual practice, we sometimes encounter obstacles. These obstacles are not external but internal; they are delusions of our own mind. The real enemy, the destroyer of our happiness, is within ourselves.

When, through training and effort, we are able to discipline and control our mind, then we will gain real peace and tranquillity.

Therefore Buddha said, "You are your own master. Everything rests on your own shoulders, depends on you."

Although, in the practice of the mind of enlightenment, we have to restrain from all negative ways, primarily we must avoid anger. Anger can never produce happiness, whereas attachment can bring about the experience of happiness in certain cases.

4. *I will learn to cherish beings of bad nature*
    And those pressed by strong sins and sufferings
    As if I had found a precious treasure
    Very difficult to find.

Some people, when they see others who are exhausted by sufferings and oppressed by delusions, tend to avoid these experiences, because they are afraid of getting involved and carried away. Bodhisattvas, instead of avoiding such situations, face them bravely and see them as an opportunity to bring happiness to other sentient beings.

5. *When others, out of jealousy, treat me badly*
    With abuse, slander, and so on,
    I will learn to take all loss
    And offer the victory to them.

When other beings, especially those who hold a grudge against you, abuse and harm you out of envy, you should not abandon them, but hold them as objects of your great compassion and take care of them.

Thus, the practitioner should take the loss on himself or herself, and offer the victory to the others.

Practitioners of the mind of enlightenment take the loss on themselves and offer the victory to others, not with the motivation of becoming virtuous themselves, but rather with the motivation to help other sentient beings.

Since it is sometimes possible, however, that taking the loss and offering the victory to others can harm them in the long run, there are cases when you should not do it.

If a practitioner of altruism finds himself in such a situation then, induced by a strong motive to help others, he should actually do the opposite.

Think in these terms. When something unpleasant happens and you get irritated, you are the loser, since irritation immediately destroys your own mental peace and in the long run brings unwanted results. Yet, if someone hurts you and you do not lose your mental peace, that is a victory.

If you become impatient and lose your temper, then you lose the best part of the human brain, judgment of the situation. Once you are angry, almost mad with anger, then you cannot make correct decisions.

When your mind is calm, you can analyse in a clearer way. Without losing your tranquillity, analyse the circumstances and, if necessary, take counter-actions. This is the spiritual meaning of loss and victory.

6. *When one whom I have benefited with great hope*
Unreasonably hurts me very badly
I will learn to view that person
As an excellent spiritual guide.

When one among those whom you have benefited repays your kindness in the wrong way, you might feel that you do not want to help him ever again. For the very reason that it is difficult not to hold this against him — and this is a great stumbling block for the practitioner of altruism — it is emphasised that a practitioner should care specially for such a person. A person who harms you should be seen not only as someone who needs your special care, but also as someone who is your spiritual guide. You will find that your enemy is your supreme teacher.

> 7. *In short, I will learn to offer to everyone*
>   *without exception*
>   *All help and happiness directly and indirectly*
>   *And respectfully take upon myself*
>   *All harm and suffering of my mothers.*

Since others are infinite in number, and since you are only one, no matter how superior you are, others become more valuable. If you have some power of judgement, you will find that it is worthwhile to sacrifice yourself for the sake of others, that one must not sacrifice infinite numbers of others for the sake of oneself.

Special visualisation is valuable here. See yourself as a very selfish person, and in front of you a great number of sentient beings undergo sufferings. Visualise them actively experiencing sufferings while you selfishly remain neutral, unbiased. Then, see which side you want to take — theirs or your own.

If selfish politicians thought like this, then they would without hesitation join the majority.

Initially, it is very difficult to decrease and control your selfish attitude. But if you persevere for a long time, you will be successful.

He who, from the depths of his heart, practises taking onto himself all the suffering and faults of other sentient beings, should also train in sharing with them all good qualities like virtues and happiness that he has in himself.

These seven verses deal with the practice of the conventional mind of enlightenment, which is method. The eighth verse deals with the practice of the ultimate mind of enlightenment, which is wisdom.

By engaging in the practice of the conventional mind of enlightenment, one accumulates a store of merit; and by engaging in the practice of the ultimate mind of enlightenment, one accumulates a store of wisdom.

With these two forces combined, one achieves as a result the two bodies of the Buddha: the Form Body, or Rupakaya; and the Truth Body, or Dharmakaya.

8. *I will learn to keep all these practices*
   Undefiled by the stains of the eight worldly
   conceptions
   And, by understanding all phenomena as
   illusions
   Be released from the bondage of attachment.

If someone undertakes such a practice motivated by worldly concerns, like wishing for a long and healthy life in which he has happiness and achieves perfection, this is basically wrong. To undertake the practice hoping that people will call one a great religious practitioner is also definitely wrong. So is viewing the objects of one's compassion as truly existent.

You should undertake this practice with the understanding that all phenomena are like illusions.

One understands that all phenomena are like illusions through negating their supposedly true existence, leaving behind what is mere imputation, label, designation. This is the Buddhist view.

Dependent arising establishes the evidence of something as not truly existent. By gaining a complete understanding of dependent arising, one has the strong conviction of the functioning of the conventions. Therefore, one engages in the practice of the mind of enlightenment and accumulates a store of merit; and by focusing on emptiness, or non-true existence, one accumulates a store of wisdom.

Supported by this strong motivation of the mind of enlightenment, one engages in the practice of the six perfections, or paramitas: generosity, discipline, patience, joyous effort, concentration and wisdom.

The six perfections can also be considered under three headings as the three higher trainings.

The first of the three higher trainings is the practice of discipline. There are three ways to effect this. The one explained in the Pratimoksha or Vinaya is called individual liberation. The second is the discipline of Bodhisattvas, and the third the discipline of Tantra.

CHAPTER 24

The Three
Higher Trainings
• •

With mind far off, not thinking of death's coming,
Performing these meaningless activities,
Returning empty-handed now would be complete
*   confusion;*
The need is recognition, the spiritual teachings,
So why not practice the path of wisdom at this
*   very moment?*
From the mouths of the saints come these words:
If you do not keep your master's teaching in your
*   heart*
Will you not become your deceiver?

— The Tibetan Book of the Dead

No matter what form of Buddhism one wishes to practice — Hinayana, Mahayana, or Vajrayana — one must begin by cultivating the Three Higher Trainings. Buddha Shakyamuni himself, whose nature was compassion, aspiring only to benefit beings, and who possessed the boundless and inconceivable jewel-like qualities of a Sugata's three special transcendences and insights, himself completed the path and taught in this way.

The doctrine that he taught is of two types: the transmission of words or the scriptures, and the transmission of insight. The latter of these refers to the inner accomplishment of the Three Higher Trainings: self-discipline, meditative concentration and wisdom. In the Hinayana, one practises these on the basis of renunciation and the aspiration to gain personal nirvana; in the Mahayana, they are practised on the basis of, and with the motivation of fulfilling, the vast Bodhisattva aspiration of gaining full Buddhahood, in order to be of maximum benefit to the world.

The first of these, the higher training in self-discipline, is said to be the basis of the other trainings and the foundation of all perfections. The Buddha himself said, "Just as the earth is the basis of life and gives birth to all that grows, likewise, discipline is the basis of those making spiritual endeavours and it gives birth to every virtue."

Also it is said, "Discipline is the staircase leading to every wholesome truth. Like the earth which is the basis for the growth of the trees, and so forth, that live upon it, discipline is the basis of all spiritual progress." The practice of discipline is advocated by all sects of Tibetan Buddhism.

Discipline is a supreme ornament and, whether worn by old, young or middle aged people, gives birth only to happiness.

What are the immediate benefits of guarding the precepts of discipline? The main function of discipline, in terms of immediately beneficial effects, is that it eliminates fallacious activities of body and speech and, consequently, one experiences pacification of coarse mental wandering to external objects, such as distraction by meaningless endeavours like overcoming enemies and protecting friends. Thus, in this very life, one gains the beneficial effect of abiding within inner joy. Through constantly possessing mindfulness, and by the power of relying upon awareness of the points of practice together with alertness, the power of samadhi is easily and quickly attained.

The second of the three higher trainings is meditative concentration, or samadhi. Discipline is the supreme fountainhead for the accomplishment of samadhi. In reliance upon the pacification of coarse mental wandering to external objects through the practice of discipline, one is spontaneously led to the sphere of thought, prepared to engage in the cultivation of purely focused absorption. At that time, one applies the methods of pacifying the subtle inner mental wanderings, such as subtle torpor and excitation, and can accomplish samatha, the essence of the training in samadhi. When this has been accomplished, one experiences the beneficial effects of being able to meditate with great strength upon any of the spiritual subjects constituting the path to higher being and enlightenment, without being distracted by subjects other than those being meditated upon. Therefore, one should strive to accomplish samatha.

As a preliminary to the actual methods of accomplishing samatha, one should abide within pure discipline while living in a solitary place conducive to mental peace. One should avoid associating with many people and eliminate the coarse conceptual mind of attraction to the objects of sensory experience.

The actual method of developing samatha is to adopt an object of concentration and pursue the process to completion. There are several types of subjects that may be used as the object of concentration: a pervasive object, an object of analytical thought, an object of wisdom, an object of purified delusion and so on. A simple, yet effective object commonly used these days is the image of the Tathagata.

Should one attain the non-conceptual blissfully clear absorption and be able to focus single-pointedly upon any subject of meditation for as long as desired, not only will one be able to meditate without distraction, but one's power of spiritual enquiry will gain unprecedented strength. One should then use this new power to engage in the training of wisdom, which investigates the egoless nature of the objects of knowledge and realises the point of spiritual investigation.

The reason for engaging in the wisdom training is that the mere accomplishment of samadhi, devoid of training in wisdom which perceives the egoless nature of every phenomenon, is not a method that is able to uproot the delusions and afflictive emotions — such as ego-grasping, the source of cyclic existence. Although one abides in samadhi for an aeon, unless it is conjoined with wisdom, one will not attain the state of liberation. Consequently, one must definitely cultivate wisdom through the understanding of egolessness. This is the remedy to eliminate all the delusions.

CHAPTER 25

Mantra

• • • • • • • • •

T he practices for maturing one's own continuum are the
six perfections, and the practices for maturing others',
the four ways of gathering students. Among the six
perfections, each of the later ones is more difficult to
achieve and is more important than the earlier ones. The
last two perfections are concentration and wisdom.

In terms of the Sutra Vehicle, there are the thirty-seven
harmonies of enlightenment for the sake of achieving
liberation, and many variations of paths for the sake
of achieving Buddhahood, as presented in Maitreyas.
For all of these, the root is the meditative stabilisation
that is a union of a calm abiding of the mind and special
insight.

As a means of achieving this meditative stabilisation, in
a quick and powerful way, there is the Mantra or Tantra
Vehicle, which comprises four Tantra sets — Action,
Performance, Yoga and Highest Yoga. The general mode
of procedure of the three lower Tantras is roughly the same,
although each has distinctive practices. In both the Perfection
Vehicle and the Secret Mantra Vehicle, the root of practice
is the altruistic intention to become enlightened and the
view of the emptiness of inherent existence, but the
greatness of Secret Mantra comes by way of meditative
stabilisation. Thus it is even said that the scriptures of Secret
Mantra are included in the sets of discourses, since
meditative stabilisation is their main topic.

In what way does the Secret Mantra Vehicle achieve its distinctiveness through meditative stabilisation? How does it have a more profound way of enhancing meditative stabilisation that is a union of calm abiding and special insight? With the altruistic intention to become enlightened, one is aiming at full enlightenment, the state of Buddhahood endowed with a Truth Body, which is the fulfilment of one's own welfare and a Form Body, which is the fulfilment of others' welfare; amongst these two, practitioners are specifically aiming more at achieving Form Bodies, in order to be of assistance to others. Form Bodies have the major and minor marks of a Buddha's body and, in the Perfection Vehicle within the Sutra system, one seeks to achieve this type of body by way of accumulating meritorious power, through practising the six perfections under the influence of great compassion and the altruistic intention to become enlightened. The distinctive feature of Mantra is, in addition to these practices, to engage in a technique that is similar in aspect to the type of Form Body that is being sought — one meditates on oneself as presently having the physical body of a Buddha, this practice being called Deity Yoga. Since what one is practising is concordant in aspect with the fruit one is trying to achieve, Deity Yoga is particularly effective and powerful.

In this way, Secret Mantra has a distinctive feature, yoga, in which the entity of method and wisdom is indivisible. In the Perfection Vehicle, the altruistic method and wisdom are separate entities that influence each other; the altruistic method is affected by the force of wisdom, and wisdom is affected by the force of the altruistic method. How does Mantra have the indivisibility of entity of the altruistic method and wisdom? In the practice of Deity Yoga, within a single consciousness, there are the two factors — of imagination of a divine body, and simultaneous ascertainment of its emptiness of inherent existence. Imagination of a divine body, which is in the class of compassionately vast appearances, helps increase the collection of merit, and hence a mind of Deity Yoga fulfils the feature of the altruistic method. Also, since this very   mind ascertains the emptiness of inherent existence of the divine body, and so on, the collection of wisdom is accumulated; thus, the same mind of Deity Yoga fulfils the qualities of wisdom. Although method and wisdom are still separable conceptually, they are contained in the entity of one consciousness.

A divine body, in this context, is one that a yogi intentionally imagines newly in meditation as an appearance — to that yogi's mental consciousness — of himself or herself in a divine body. Thus, it seems that, when yogis imagine themselves as being a deity and realise the emptiness of inherent existence of that divine body, there must be a difference in the impact on the consciousness of this special object, which is the substratum of emptiness.

Also when, in the Perfection Vehicle, one meditates on the emptiness of the self and the phenomena included in the five aggregates, one does not engage in techniques to cause the substratum — the emptiness of which is the object of meditation — to keep appearing and not to disappear. In the Mantra system, one specifically trains in keeping the appearance of the divine body in the midst of ascertaining its emptiness of inherent existence. Thus, there has to be a difference from this point of view also. Since, within the imagining of a divine body, the mode of apprehension of the same consciousness ascertains the emptiness of the inherent existence of that body, it is said that a factor of the wisdom-consciousness realising emptiness appears as a deity.

Highest Yoga Tantra

In Highest Yoga Tantra, there is an even more profound way in which the entity of altruistic method and wisdom are undifferentiable. This comes by way of focusing on more subtle physical and mental factors — the very subtle wind, or energy, and the very subtle mind, which themselves are undifferentiable entities. To practise this level, it is necessary to forcefully stop the coarser levels of wind and mind — and many different techniques for practicing this, by putting concentrated emphasis on different places in the body, are described in Higher Yoga Tantras. This is the practice of the channels, the winds, or internal energies, and the drops of essential fluid.

In general, the cultivation of special insight involves analytical meditation but, due to these special factors, in Highest Yoga Tantra it is stabilising meditation that is emphasised when cultivating special insight. Coarser levels of consciousness induce ascertainment through analysis and investigation, but when one purposely manifests subtler levels of consciousness — not at times when these happen naturally due to the power of karma, such as while dying, but when they are induced through the power of yoga — these subtle consciousnesses in which the coarser levels have ceased are fully capable of ascertaining meanings. If one engages in analysis at that time, it causes the subtler level to cease and a coarser level to return. Since the subtler level of mind compensates for analysis — the purpose of which is to endow the mind with the capability of profound ascertainment — one does not analyse at that time, and stabilising meditation is prescribed.

Concerning the mode of meditation in Highest Yoga Tantra, there are two main systems for achieving a Buddha body — through focusing on both very subtle wind and mind, and through focusing only on very subtle mind. In most of the Highest Yoga Tantras of the New Translation Schools, such as Guhyasamaja, Chakrasamvara, and so on, the emphasis is on both very subtle wind and mind in order to achieve a Buddha body. However, in the Kalachakra system, the emphasis is only on very subtle mind; and in the practice of the Great Seal and the Great Completeness, the emphasis is also mainly on very subtle mind.

From another perspective, it is said that, among Highest Yoga Tantras, one group focuses on the channels, winds and drops of essential fluids, in order to manifest the fundamental innate mind of clear light; and another manifests that mind through sustaining only a non-conceptual state without focusing on channels, winds and drops. Within the first, there are Tantras that put particular emphasis on the wind-yoga, as is the case with Guhyasamaga and Tantras that put particular emphasis on the four joys, as is the case with Chakrasamvara. The Great Seal and the Great Completeness are among those that manifest the fundamental innate mind of clear light, through sustaining only a non-conceptual state.

Prior to engaging in the practice of Mantra, it is necessary to receive initiation and, after receiving initiation, it is important to keep the pledges and the vows. In initiation, one person transmits a lineage of blessing to another, and even though blessings can be gained from reading books and so forth, there is a difference when a blessing is received from a living person's mental continuum, in that its benefit forms more easily in the mind. Due to this, in Secret Mantra, lamas are valued highly.

CHAPTER 26

Mind Transformation through Meditation

• •

Rest in natural great peace
This exhausted mind
Beaten helpless by karma and neurotic thought
Like the relentless fury of the pounding waves
In the infinite ocean of samsara.
— Nyoshul Khenpo

Meditation is a familiarisation of the mind with an object of meditation. In terms of how the mind is familiarised with the object, there are many types of meditation. In one type, the mind is generated into the entity of a particular type of consciousness, as in meditating compassion or meditating wisdom. In such meditation, you are seeking to generate your own mind into a compassionate consciousness or a wisdom consciousness — compassion and wisdom not being the object on which you are meditating, but that entity into which you are seeking to transform your consciousness, through a process of familiarisation.

However, when you meditate on impermanence and selflessness, they are taken as the objects of the mode of apprehension of the mind, and you are meditating them. In another type of meditation, if you meditate on the good qualities of a Buddha, wishing to attain them, these qualities are the objects of wishing; this is called meditation in the manner of wishing. Another type of meditation is one in which you cause levels of the path to appear to the mind, in the sense of talking to the mind, saying that there are such and such levels of realisation: this is called reflective meditation.

In another way, meditation is divided into two types: analytical and stabilising. In general, calm abiding (samatha), is stabilising meditation, whereas special insight (vipashyana) is analytical meditation.

With respect to objects of meditation, the objects of both stabilising and analytical meditation can be either the final mode of being of phenomena, or any among the varieties of phenomena. In general, emptiness is something found at the conclusion of analysis by reasoning investigating the final mode of being of objects; nevertheless, at the time of stabilising meditation observing emptiness, the meditator fixes one-pointedly on the meaning of emptiness which has been ascertained, and does not analyse. Thus, there is both stabilising and analytical meditation; observing any of the varieties of phenomena can occur, depending on how the mind is acting on the object.

Calm abiding, which is predominantly stabilising meditation, is common to both non-Buddhists and Buddhists. Within Buddhism, it is common to both the low and great vehicles and, within the great vehicle, is common to both the Sutra and Mantra Vehicles.

Our mind as it is now, is completely scattered and attached to external objects, due to which it is powerless. Our thought is like water running in every direction. But just as water, when channelised, becomes powerful, so it is with our minds.

How is the mind channelised? In the Mantra Vehicle in general, and in Highest Yoga Mantra in particular, many techniques are described, but first I will describe the technique that is common to all vehicles. In order to set the mind steadily on an object of observation, it is necessary initially to identify an object of observation. The Buddha described four types of objects for purifying behaviour. No matter what afflictive emotion we predominantly engaged in earlier, its force remains with our mind now, and thus it is necessary to choose an object for meditation which will counter the force of that particular afflictive emotion. For someone who predominantly engaged in desire, the object of meditation is ugliness. Meditating on ugliness means to investigate the nature of our physical body.

For someone who has predominantly engaged in hatred, the object of meditation is love. For someone who was predominantly sunk in obscuration, the meditation is on the twelve links of the dependent-arising of cyclic existence. For someone whose predominant afflictive emotion is pride, the meditation should be on the divisions of the constituents because, when meditating on the many divisions, you get to the point where you realise that there are many things you do not know, thereby lessening pride. For those dominated by conceptuality, the prescribed meditation is on observing the exhalation and inhalation of the breath. These are the objects for purifying behaviour.

As mentioned earlier, the object of observation could also be emptiness. Also, you could take even a flower, and so on, as the object. Still another is to take your own mind as the object of observation. Also, a Buddhist could meditate on Buddha's body; a Christian could meditate on Jesus or the cross.

No matter what the object is, it is not a case of meditating within, looking at an external object with your eyes, but of causing an image of it to appear to the mental conciousness. This image is called a reflection, and it is the object of observation.

Having identified the object, how do you set your mind on it? Initially, you have to hear about the object to be meditated on from a teacher; then, you gain ascertainment of it by thinking again and again about it. For instance, if you are to meditate on the body of a Buddha, you first need to come to know it through hearing it described, or looking at a picture or statue, and then get used to it — so that it can appear clearly to the mind.

At that point, imagine it about four feet in front of you, at the height of your eyebrows. It should be meditated on as clear, with a nature of light; this helps to prevent the onset of laxity. Also, consider the imagined Buddha body to be heavy; this helps to prevent excitement. The more you can reduce the size of the object, the more it helps in withdrawing the mind, channelising it. Your physical posture is also important.

While meditating on the object, your mind must have two qualities: great clarity, not only of the object but also of the consciousness; and abiding one-pointedly on the object of observation. Two opposite factors prevent these from developing — laxity and excitement. Laxity prevents the development of clarity, and excitement prevents the stability of staying with the object.

Laxity is a case of the mind becoming too relaxed, too loose, lacking intensity — the mind having lost its tautness. A cause of laxity is lethargy, which is like a hat on the head, a feeling of heaviness. As an antidote, you have to make the mind more taut.

When the mode of apprehension of the mind is tightened, there is less danger of laxity, but more danger of generating excitement. Scattering of the mind due to desire is called excitement; thus, scattering can be to any type of objects, whereas excitement is a scattering only to objects of desire. As an antidote to excitement and any other type of scattering, you need to lower the level of the mode of apprehension of the mind, making it less taut.

While holding the object of observation with mindfulness, investigate with introspection from time to time, to see whether the mind has come under the influence of laxity or excitement. If, through introspection, you find that there is danger of laxity, you need to heighten the mode of apprehension a little. Through experience, a sense of a moderate level of tautness of the mind will develop.

To heighten the level of the mode of apprehension of the mind, reflect on something that makes you joyous; to lower it, reflect on something that sobers the mind, such as suffering. When initially training this way, it is best to do frequent, short sessions of meditation and, because it is difficult initially to generate a deep state of meditation when in a busy and noisy city, you need complete isolation and tranquillity. Without quiet, it is almost impossible to achieve a fully qualified state of calm abiding.

As you practice in this way, the mind gradually develops more and more stability, culminating in calm abiding. Through the power of stabilising meditation, in which the mind is set one-pointedly on its object of observation, mental pliancy is generated, leading to the bliss of physical pliancy. In dependence upon that, the bliss of mental pliancy is generated. At the point at which the bliss of mental pliancy becomes stable, calm abiding is achieved.

Special insight is attained in a similar way when the bliss of mental pliancy is induced, not by the power of stabilising meditation, but by the power of analysis with investigatory wisdom. There are mundane and supramundane forms of special insight. The mundane is a case of viewing a lower level as gross and a higher level as peaceful, whereas supramundane special insight, if taken in a general way, has the aspect of the Four Noble Truths. From the specific viewpoint of the Great Vehicle systems of tenets, supramundane special insight has the aspect of the selflessness of phenomena.

With regard to mantras that one can observe in meditation, there are external sounds of oral repetition. There are also natural self-arisen sounds, such as the appearance of the inhalation and exhalation of breath as tones of the mantra.

While meditating on the sound of the mantra, if it is comfortable for you to do so, imagine that you are in the middle of this, like in the house of your body. If you have a sense of the main part of consciousness being around the eyes, it is possible to imagine the light behind the eyes and then, strongly identifying yourself as being there in the middle of that light, move the light and consciousness down to the centre of the mantra circle, which is at the heart. If you do this many times, you will gradually have the sense that you are right here in the heart. Then, with you in the centre of the mantra, it will seem as if you are reading the letters of the mantra around you, not orally but mentally — reciting the mantra, but not with the mouth. There are many different techniques.

Five faults are explained as obstacles to meditation. The first is laziness; the second is to forget the advice on the object — that is, to forget the object; next are laxity and excitement; then, failure to apply an antidote when laxity and excitement are present; and the last is to continue applying the antidotes when laxity and excitement have already been overcome. These are called the five faults. Eight antidotes are given for them. The antidotes to laziness are, first of all, the Faith that intelligently sees the value of meditative stabilisation, the prime value being that without it the higher paths cannot be generated. In dependence upon ascertaining the good qualities of meditative stabilisation, the Aspiration which seeks to attain those qualities is induced. By means of that, Exertion comes, whereby you eventually attain Pliancy, causing body and mind to be free from unfavourable states and to be serviceable in a virtuous direction, so that whichever virtue is practised is powerful. These four are the antidotes to the first fault, laziness.

It is helpful not to practise too long in the beginning; do not over-extend yourself — the maximum period is around fifteen minutes. The important thing is not the length of the session, but the quality of it. If you meditate too long, you can become sleepy, and then your meditation will become a matter of becoming accustomed to that state. This is not only a waste of time, but also a habit that is difficult to eliminate in the future. In the beginning, start with many short sessions — even eight to sixteen sessions in a day —and then, as you get used to the process of meditation, the quality will improve, and the sessions will naturally become longer.

A sign that your meditative stabilisation is progressing well is that, even though your meditative sessions may be long, it will feel as though only a short time has passed. If it seems that you have spent a long time in meditation even though you have spent only a little time, this is a sign that you should shorten the length of the session.

CHAPTER 27

Science and Spirituality
● ●

I feel that the topic of the relation between matter and consiousness is a place where Eastern philosophy — particularly Buddhist philosophy — and western science could meet. I think this should be a happy marriage, with no divorce! If we work along the lines of a joint effort by Buddhist scholars — not mere scholars, but those who also have some experience — and pure unbiased physicists, to investigate, study and engage in deeper research in the field of the relation between matter and consciousness, by the next century we may find beautiful things that may be helpful. This does not have to be considered the practice of religion, but can be engaged in simply for the extension of human knowledge.

Also, the scientists who are working in the field of the neurology of the human brain could benefit from Buddhist explanations about consciousness — how it functions, how it changes in terms of levels, and so on.

Because of Buddhism's emphasis on self-creation, there is no creator deity, and thus, from this viewpoint, some people consider it, strictly speaking, not a religion. A western Buddhist scholar told me, "Buddhism is not a religion; it is a kind of science of mind." In this sense, Buddhism does not belong to the category of religion. I consider this to be unfortunate, but in any case it means that Buddhism gets closer to science. Furthermore, from the pure scientist's viewpoint, Buddhism is naturally considered a type of spiritual path. Again, it is unfortunate that it does not belong to the category of science.

Buddhism, therefore, belongs to neither religion nor pure science, but this situation provides us with an opportunity to make a link, or a bridge, between faith and science. In order to achieve the maximum happiness and satisfaction, we need to understand everything that is connected with mankind and its quest for happiness, whether it be in the field of matter or in the spiritual field. Then, taking advantage of our knowledge of the different approaches, we have to find the right method to follow, in order to achieve that aim.

The knowledge of external phenomena, and the application of that knowledge, is what we nowadays call science. The approach and methods which focus primarily on internal phenomena — consciousness or the mind — constitute another sphere of knowledge. Both have the same objective, the achievement of happiness and satisfaction, which are the intimate concern of every human being. Not only the objective, but the method is also directly related to human beings, as it is the individual person who puts it into action. The scientist investigating external phenomena is still a living human being who wants happiness; whether it is his profession or not, consciousness is also his concern. The spiritual person, whose interest lies in consciousness, or meditation, has to deal with matter. No one single way is sufficient; indeed if just one approach had been found to be so, the need would never have been felt to bring these disciplines together. Both approaches are therefore very important.

The fundamental view or philosophy of Buddhism is that of dependent arising. When one talks about the view of dependent arising, one means that things exist in dependence, or that they are imputed depending on something or the other. In the case of a physical phenomenon, one would specify that it exists in dependence on its parts, whereas non-physical composite phenomena would be described as existing in dependence either on their continuity or an aspect of their continuity. Consequently, whether it is external or internal phenomena, there is nothing that exists, except in dependence upon its parts or aspects.

If one were to investigate to find a basis for the imputation in any given phenomenon — since one would not find anything at all which is actually the phenomenon, no solid lump of anything that one could point one's finger at, which represents the phenomenon — then one says that phenomena exist through the imputation of the mind.

As phenomena do not exist independently of the imputing mind, one speaks of emptiness, which means the lack of any intrinsic existence that does not depend upon the imputing mind. Since things do not exist just of their own accord, but in dependence on conditions, they change whenever they encounter different conditions. Thus, they come into existence in dependence on conditions and they cease in dependence on conditions. That very lack of any intrinsic existence, independent of cause and conditions, is the basis for all the changes that are possible in a phenomenon, such as birth, cessation and so on.

It may be interesting to compare the scientific interpretation of the role of the observer or participator with the Buddhist view that observed phenomena do not exist merely as a mental image, a projection or vision of the mind, but rather as separate entities from the mind. Mind and matter are two separate things. Matter is separate from the mind which cognizes it and denominates it. This means that, with regard to all phenomena without exception — though they are not simply a creation or manifestation of the mind with no entity of their own — their ultimate mode of existence is dependent on the mind that imputes them, the imputer. Their mode of existence is therefore quite separate from the imputer, but their existence itself is dependent on the imputer. This point of view perhaps corresponds to the scientific explanation of the role of the observer. Though different terms are employed to explain them, their meanings are somewhat related.

On the surface, dependent arising and emptiness may seem quite contrary. Yet, if one analyses them at a much deeper level, one can come to understand that phenomena, on account of their being empty, are dependently arising or dependently existing; and, because of that dependent existence, are empty by nature. Thus, one can establish both emptiness and dependent arising on one single basis; and two faces which, at a general level, seem to be contradictory, when understood at a very profound level, will be seen to fit together in a very complementary fashion.

The mode of existence of phenomena is differentiated from their mode of appearance. Phenomena appear to the mind differently from their actual mode of existence.

When the mind apprehends their way of appearing, accepts that appearance as true, and follows that particular idea or concept, then one makes mistakes. Since that concept is completely distorted in its apprehension of the object, it contradicts the actual mode of existence, or reality itself. So this disparity or contradiction between what is and what appears is due to the fact that, although phenomena are in reality empty of any intrinsic nature, yet they do appear to the ordinary mind as if they exist inherently, though they lack any such quality. Similarly, although, in reality, things which depend on causes are impermanent and transient, undergoing constant change, they do appear as though they were permanent and unchanging. Again, something that in its true nature is suffering, appears as happiness. And something which is in reality false appears as true. There are many levels of subtlety regarding this contradiction between the mode of existence of phenomena and their mode of appearance. As a result of the contradiction between what is and what appears, all manner of mistakes are made. This explanation may have much in common with scientists' views of the difference in the modes of appearance and existence of certain phenomena.

Generally speaking, an understanding of the meaning of emptiness and dependent arising will naturally lead one to a deeper conviction in the law of cause and effect — where, as a result of different causes and conditions, corresponding fruits or effects — positive or negative — arise. One will then pay more attention to the causes and also be more aware of the various conditions. If one has a good understanding of emptiness, or familiarity with it, then the arising of distortions — like attachment, hatred, and so on — in the mind will diminish, since they are caused by a mistaken view, mistaken in not correctly distinguishing between what is and what appears. We can see, for instance, from own experience, how our feeling towards something we observe changes, depending on our state of mind. Although the object remains the same, our reaction will be far less intense when our mind is calm, than if it is overcome by some strong emotional feeling, like anger. The actual mode of existence of phenomena, the bare truth of existence, is emptiness. When one understands this, and appreciates the contradictory nature of the appearance of phenomena, one will immediately be able to realise this mistaken view to be untrue. Consequently, all mental distortions such as attachment, hatred, and so on, which are based on that misconception — a deception rooted in the contradictory nature of phenomena — will decrease in strength.

We might ask, "How do the different levels of the consciousness or mind that apprehends an object actually come to exist themselves? Different levels of consciousness are established in relation to the different levels of subtlety of the inner energy that activates and moves the consciousness towards a given object. So, the level of their subtlety and strength in moving the consciousness towards the object determines and establishes the different levels of consciousness.

It is very important to reflect upon the relationship between the inner consciousness and outer material substances. Many eastern philosophies, and Buddhism in particular, speak of four elements: earth, water, fire and air; or five elements, with the addition of space. The first four elements — earth, water, fire and air — are supported by the elements of space, which enables them to exist and function. Space or ether serves, then, as the basis for the functioning of all the other elements.

These five elements can be divided into two types: the outer five elements and the inner five elements. There is a definite relationship between the outer and inner elements. As regards the element space or ether, according to certain Buddhists texts, such as the Kalachakra Tantra, space is not just a total voidness, devoid of anything at all, but it is referred to in terms of empty particles. These empty particles therefore serve as the basis for the evolution and dissolution of the other four elements. They are generated from it and finally absorbed back into it.

The process of dissolution evolves in this order: earth, water, fire and air; and the process of generation in this order: air, fire, water and earth. These four are better understood in terms of solidity (earth), liquidity (water), heat (fire), and energy (air). The four elements are generated from the subtle level to the gross, out of this basis of empty particles, and dissolve from the gross level to the subtle into the empty particles. Space, or the empty particle, is the basis for the whole process. The Big-Bang model of the beginning of the universe perhaps has something in common with this empty particle. Such parallels do present something that I feel it would be worthwhile to reflect upon.

From the spiritual point of view of Buddhism, the state of our mind, whether it is disciplined or undisciplined, produces what is known as karma. This is accepted in many eastern philosophies. Karma, meaning action, has a particular influence upon the inner elements, which in turn affect the outer elements. This, too, is a point for further investigation.

Another area in Tibetan Buddhism, which may be of interest to scientists, is the relationship between the physical elements and the nerves, and consciousness; in particular, the relationship between the elements in the brain and consciousness. Involved here are the changes in consciousness, happy or unhappy states of mind and so on, the kind of effect they have on the elements within the brain; and the consequent effect on the body. Certain physical illnesses improve or worsen according to the state of mind. Regarding this kind of relationship between body and mind, Buddhism can definitely make a contribution to modern science.

Buddhism also explains, with great precision, the different levels of subtlety within consciousness itself. These are very clearly described in the Tantras. Consciousness is classified, from the point of view of its levels of subtlety, into three levels: the waking state or the gross level of consciousness; the consciousness of the dream state, which is more subtle; and consciousness during deep, dreamless sleep, which is subtler still.

Similarly, the three stages of birth, death and the intermediate state are also established in terms of the subtlety of their levels of consciousness. During the process of dying, a person experiences the innermost, subtle consciousness; the consciousness becomes grosser after death in the intermediate state, and progressively more gross during the process of birth. Upon the basis of the continuity of the stream of consciousness is established the existence of rebirth and re-incarnation. There are currently a number of well-documented cases of individuals who clearly remember their past lives, and it would seem very worthwhile to investigate these phenomena, with a view to expanding human knowledge.

CHAPTER 28

The Buddhist Concept of Nature

N agarjuna said that, in a system where emptiness is possible, it is also possible to have every functionality; and since functionality is possible, emptiness is possible. When we talk about nature, ultimate nature is emptiness. What is meant by emptiness, or shunyata? It is not the emptiness of existence, but rather the emptiness of true or independent existence, which means that things exist in dependence upon other factors. So, whether it is the environment that is inhabited, or the inhabitants, both of them are composed of four or five basic elements. These elements are earth, wind, fire, water and vacuum, that is space.

In the Kalachakra Tantra, there is a mention of what is known as the atom of space, particles of space. So that forms the central force of the entire phenomenon. When the whole system of the universe first evolved, it evolved from this central force, which is the particle of space; similarly, the whole system of the universe will also dissolve eventually into this particle of space. It is on the basis of these five basic elements that there is a very close inter-relatedness, or inter-relation, between the habitat, that is the natural environment; and the inhabitants, the sentient beings living within it.

There are also internal elements which are existent inherently within sentient beings; they are of different levels — some are subtle and some are gross.

Ultimately, according to Buddhist teachings, the innermost subtle consciousness is the sole sort of creator, itself consisting of five elements, very subtle forms of elements. These subtle elements serve as conditions for producing the internal elements which form sentient beings, and that in turn causes the existence or evolution of the external elements. So, there is a very close inter-dependence, or inter-relationship, between the environment and the inhabitants. Within the meaning of interdependence, there are many different levels — that things are dependent upon their causal factors, or upon their own parts, or on the conceptual mind which actually gives the label designation.

All religions agree that we cannot find lasting inner satisfaction based on selfish desires and acquiring the comforts of material things. Even if we could, there are now so many people, that the earth would not sustain us for long. I think it is much better to practice enjoying simple peace of mind. We can share the earth and take care of it together, rather than trying to posses it, destroying the beauty of life in the process.

In the context of Buddhism, trees are often mentioned in accounts of the principal events of our teacher, Buddha Shakyamuni's life. He was born as his mother leaned against a tree for support. He attained enlightenment seated beneath a tree, and finally passed away as trees stood witness overhead. According to the vinaya, their code of discipline, fully-ordained monks are enjoined not only to avoid cutting trees, but also to plant and nurture them. Therefore, we can conclude that to plant and nurture trees is an act of virtue. Moreover, in addition to providing homes for birds and animals, trees are described in the scriptures as the abode of deities, nagas and local spirits. These are further reasons to protect them.

Just as trees, particularly fruit trees, are valued for their contribution to our physical health, flowers have a soothing effect on the mind. We decorate our places of worship with them and invariably make offerings of them in our religious rituals. In the Buddhist tradition, we do not even need to pick or own them — simply looking at flowers and offering them in our imagination is a powerful means of accumulating merit. When people are under stress, when their minds are disturbed, sitting or strolling in a garden can bring refreshment and peace.

I always try to express the value of having a good heart. This simple aspect of human nature can be nourished and given great power. With a good heart and wisdom we will have the right motivation and will automatically do what needs to be done. If people begin to act with genuine compassion for everyone, we can still protect each other and the natural environment. This is much easier than having to adapt to the severe and incomprehensible environmental conditions projected for the future.

Basically, we all cherish tranquillity. For example, when spring comes, the days grow longer, there is more sunshine, the grass and the trees come alive and everything is fresh. People feel happy. In autumn, one leaf falls, then another, then all the beautiful flowers die, until we are surrounded by bare naked plants. We do not feel so joyful. Why is this? Because deep down, we desire constructive, fruitful growth and dislike things collapsing, dying or being destroyed. Every destructive action goes against our basic nature; building, being constructive, is the human way.

Now, on close examination, the human mind, the human heart and the environment are inseparably linked together. If you develop concern for other people's welfare, share other people's sufferings, and help them, ultimately you will benefit. If you think only of yourself and forget about others, ultimately you will lose.

CHAPTER 29

Dharma and Politics

●●●●●●●●●●●●●●●●●●●●●●●●●●●●●●

H appiness is man's prerogative. He seeks it, and each man is equally entitled to his pursuit of happiness. No man seeks misery. Justice and equality are man's prerogatives too; but they should derive their practice from altruism and not have been corroded by the stations of power and wealth. In order to develop such an altruistic motivation, that justice and equality may co-exist in truth, the creation of a staunch moral fabric for the social environment is a prerequisite. Concerned voices are being raised about this inherent vacuum in the moral foundation — the foremost deterrent to a just and equal world.

Not only must the entire social structure undergo a dynamic metamorphosis, but the chief constituent of this structure — the caretaker of society, man — must re-evaluate his attitudes, principles and values in order that such a change is seriously effected. Sceptics might question the possibility of altering the social system; but are we not the makers of our own environment? Man has created his social dilemmas, and if any change is to happen, the power to make it happen lies with man alone.

Man and society are interdependent — hence the quality of man's behaviour as an individual and as a participant in his society is inseparable. Reparations have been attempted in the past as contributions to lessening the malaise and dysfunctional attitudes of our social world — in order to build a society which is more just and equal.

Institutions and organisations have been established, with their charters of noble ideology, to combat these social problems. For all intents and purposes, the objectives have been laudable; but it has been unfortunate that basically good ideas have been defeated by man's self-interest. Today, ethics and moral principles sadly fail in the field of political culture.

There is a school of thought which warns the moralist to refrain from politics, as politics is devoid of ethics and moral principles. This is a wrong approach, since politics devoid of ethics does not further the benefits to man and his society — and life without morality will make men no better than beasts. The political concept is not axiomatically dirty, a common adjective ascribed to politics today; but the instruments of our political culture have tampered with and distorted the fundamental concepts of fine ideals, to further their own selfish ends. Today, spiritual people are voicing their concern about the intermingling of politics with religion, since they fear the violation of ethics by politics, contaminating the purity of religion. This line of thought is both selfish and contradictory. All religions exist to serve and help man and any divorce from politics forsakes a powerful instrument for social welfare. Religion and politics are a useful combination for the welfare of man, when tempered by correct ethical concepts, with a minimum of self-interest.

In the correlation between ethics and politics, should deep moral convictions form the guideline for the political practitioner, man and society will reap far-reaching benefits. It is an absurd assumption that religion and morality have no place in politics, and that men of religion, believers in morality should seclude themselves, or become hermits. These ideas lack proper perspective on man's relation to society and the role of politics in our lives. Strong morality and ethics are as crucial to a man of politics as they are to a man of religion, for dangerous consequences are foreseen when our politicians, and those who rule, forget their moral principles and convictions.

Irrespective of whether we are believers or agnostics, whether we believe in God or karma, moral ethics is a code which everyone is able to follow. We need human qualities such as moral scruples, compassion and humility. In recognition of human frailty and weakness, these qualities are only accessible through forceful individual development in a conducive social milieu, so that a more humane world can come into being — this is the ultimate goal. Realisation that materialism does not foster the growth of morals, compassion and humility should be created and arise within man. The functional importance of religious and social institutions promoting these qualities cannot be over-estimated.

This is a serious responsibility and all efforts should be concentrated sincerely towards fulfilling these needs. Prejudice and bias should be forgotten, and different religions should work in unity, not only for the creation of these qualities in man, but also for an atmosphere of harmony and understanding. In terms of communications, the world has become appreciably smaller today; and with respect to its limitations, no nation can survive in isolation. It is in our own interest to create a world of love, justice and equality; because, without a sense of universal responsibility based on morality, our existence and survival is at a perilous precipice.

The qualities required to create such a world must be inculcated right from the beginning, when the child is young. We cannot expect our generation or the new generation to make the change without this basic foundation. If there is any hope, it is in the future generation, but not unless we initiate a major change in our present educational system on a worldwide basis.

A dynamic revolution is deemed crucial for inculating a political culture in morality and ethics. Such a revolution must be sponsored by the powerful nations, for any such attempt by the smaller and the weaker nations is unlikely to succeed. If powerful nations adopt policies based on a bedrock of moral principles and, if they concern themselves genuinely with the welfare of mankind, a new path and a new hope will emerge. Such a revolution will surpass all other attempts to achieve justice and equality in our world.

CHAPTER 30

Religious Harmony

●●●●●●●●●●●●●●●●●●●●●●●●●●●

A mong spiritual faiths, there are many different philosophies, some dramatically opposite to each other on certain points. Buddhists do not accept a creator; Christians base their philosophy on that theory. All the different religious communities accept that there is another force beyond the reach of our ordinary senses. When we pray together, there is a certain feeling that we can experience. If we utilise it properly, that feeling is very helpful for the generation of inner strength. For a real sense of brotherhood and sisterhood, that feeling — that atmosphere and experience — is very useful and helpful.

All the different religious faiths, despite their philosophical differences, have a similar objective. Every religion emphasises human improvement, love, respect for others, sharing other people's suffering. On these lines, every religion has more or less the same viewpoint and the same goal.

Those faiths which emphasise almighty God — and faith in and love of God — have as their purpose the fulfilment of God's intentions. Seeing us all as creation, and followers, of one God, they teach that we should cherish and help each other. The very purpose of faithful belief in God is to accomplish his wishes, the essence of which is to cherish, respect, love and be of service to our fellow humans.

Since an essential purpose of other religions is similarly to promote such beneficial feelings and actions, I strongly feel that, from this viewpoint, the central purpose of all the different philosophical explanations are the same. Through the various religious systems, followers are assuming a salutary attitude toward their fellow humans—our brothers and sisters—and implementing this good motivation in the service of human society. This has been demonstrated by a great many believers in Christianity throughout history; many have sacrificed their lives for the benefit of humankind. This is true implementation of compassion.

Love and kindness are the very basis of society. If we lose these feelings, society will face tremendous difficulties; the survival of humanity will be endangered. Together with material development, we need spiritual development, so that inner peace and social harmony can be experienced. Without inner peace, without inner calm, it is difficult to have lasting peace. In this field of inner development, religion can make important contributions.

Although, in every religion, there is an emphasis on compassion and love, from the viewpoint of philosophy, there are differences, and that is all right. Philosophical teachings are not the end, not the aim, not what you serve. The aim is help and benefit others, and philosophical teachings that support those ideas are valuable. If we go into the differences in philosophy and argue with and criticize each other, it is useless. There will be endless argument; the only result will be that we irritate each other— accomplishing nothing. It is better to look at the purpose of the philosophies and to see what is shared — an emphasis on love, compassion and respect for a higher force.

No religion basically believes that material progress alone is sufficient for humankind. All religions believe in forces beyond material progress. All agree that it is very important and worthwhile to make a strong effort to serve human society.

Just as the Buddha was an example of contentment, tolerance, and serving others without selfish motivation, so was Jesus Christ. Almost all the great teachers lived a saintly life — not luxuriously like kings or emperors, but as simple human beings. Their inner strength was tremendous, limitless, but the external appearance was of contentment with a simple way of life.

The motivation of all religious practices is similar — love, sincerity, honesty. The way of life of practically all religious persons rests in contentment. The teachings of tolerance, love and compassion are the same. A basic goal is the benefit of humankind — each system seeking in its own unique way to improve human beings. If we put too much emphasis on our own philosophy, religion or theory, are too attached to it, and try to impose it on other people, it causes trouble. Basically, all the great teachers, such as Gautama Buddha, Jesus Christ or Mohammed, founded their new teachings with a motivation of helping their fellow humans. They did not mean to gain anything for themselves, or to create more trouble or unrest in the world.

It is more important that we respect each other and learn from each other especially those things that will enrich our own practice. Even if all the systems are separate, since they have the same goal, the study of each other's faiths is helpful.

The variety of global religious philosophies is a very useful and beautiful thing. For certain people, the idea of God as creator, and of everything depending on his will, is beneficial and soothing and so, for that person, such a doctrine is worthwhile. For someone else, the idea that there is no creator, that ultimately, one is oneself the creator— in that everything depends upon oneself — is more appropriate. For certain people, it may be a more effective method of spiritual growth, it may be more beneficial. For such persons, this idea is better and for the other type of person, the other idea is more suitable.

CHAPTER 31

Universal Responsibility

● ●

T his idea of universal responsibility is rooted in a very simple fact — in general terms, all others' desires are the same as mine. Every being wants happiness and does not want suffering. If we, as intelligent human beings, do not accept this fact, there will be more and more suffering on this planet. If we adopt a self-centred approach to life, and constantly try to use others for our own self-interest, we may gain temporary benefits but, in the long run, we will not succeed in achieving even personal happiness; and world peace will be completely out of the question.

In their quest for happiness, humans have used different methods, which have all too often been cruel and repellent. Behaving in ways utterly unbecoming to their status as humans, they inflict suffering upon fellow humans and other living beings, for their own selfish gains. In the end, such short-sighted actions bring suffering to oneself as well as to others. To be born a human being is a rare event in itself, and it is wise to use this opportunity as effectively and skilfully as possible. We must have the proper perspective, that of the universal life process, so that the happiness or glory of one person or group is not sought at the expense of others.

All this calls for a new approach to global problems. The world is becoming smaller and smaller— and more and more interdependent—as a result of rapid technological advances and international trade, as well as increasing trans-national relations. We now depend very much on each other. In ancient times, problems were mostly family size, and they were naturally tackled at the family level, but the situation has changed. Today, we are so interdependent, so closely interconnected with each other that, without a sense of universal responsibility, a feeling of universal brotherhood and an understanding and belief that we really are part of one big human family, we cannot hope to overcome the dangers to our very existence — let alone bring about peace and happiness.

Nature's law dictates that, in order to survive, bees must work together. As a result, they instinctively possess a sense of social responsibility. They have no constitution, no law, no police, no religion or moral training but, because of their nature, they labour faithfully together. Occasionally, they may fight, but in general, based on cooperation, the whole colony survives. We human beings have a constitution, laws and a police force. We have religion, remarkable intelligence and hearts with a great capacity to love. We have many extraordinary qualities but, in actual practice, I think we are behind those small insects. In some ways, I feel that we are poorer than the bees.

For instance, millions of people live together, all over the world, in large cities. Despite such proximity, many are lonely. Unfortunately, though we are social animals compelled to coexist, we greatly lack a sense of responsibility for our fellow human beings.

One nation's problems can no longer be satisfactorily solved by itself alone; too much depends on the interest, attitude and cooperation of other nations. A universal humanitarian approach to world problems seems the only basis for world peace. What does this mean? We begin from the recognition referred to earlier that all beings cherish happiness and do not want suffering. It then becomes both morally wrong and pragmatically unwise to pursue only one's own happiness, oblivious to the feelings and aspirations of all others who surround us as members of the same human family. The wiser course is to also think of others when pursuing our own happiness. This will lead to what I call wise self-interest, which hopefully will transform itself into cooperative self-interest or, better still, mutual interest.

Although the increasing interdependence among nations might be expected to generate more sympathetic cooperation, it is difficult to achieve a spirit of genuine cooperation, as long as people remain indifferent to the feelings and happiness of others. When people are motivated mostly by greed and jealousy, it is not possible for them to live in harmony. A spiritual approach may not solve all the political problems that have been caused by the existing self-centred approach but, in the long run, it will overcome the very basis of the problems that we face today.

On the other hand, if humankind continues to approach its problems considering only temporary expediency, future generations will have to face tremendous difficulties.

Adopting an attitude of universal responsibility is essentially a personal matter. Their real test of compassion is not what we say in abstract discussions, but how we conduct ourselves in daily life. Still, certain fundamental views are basic to the practice of altruism.

Though no system of goverment is perfect, democracy is closest to humanity's essential nature. Hence, those of us who enjoy it must continue to fight for all people's right to do so. Furthermore, democracy is the only stable foundation upon which a global political structure can be built. To work as one, we must respect the right of all peoples and nations to maintain their own distinctive character and values.

We also need to renew our commitment to human values in the field of modern science. Though the main purpose of science is to learn more about reality, another of its goals is to improve the quality of life. Without altruistic motivation, scientists cannot distinguish between beneficial technologies and those that are merely expedient. The environmental damage surrounding us is the most obvious example of the result of this confusion, but proper motivation may be even more relevant in guiding and governing how we handle the extraordinary new array of biological technologies with which we can now manipulate the subtle structures of life itself. If we do not base every action on an ethical foundation, we run the risk of inflicting terrible harm on the delicate matrix of life.

Nor are the religions of the world exempt from this responsibility. The purpose of religion is not to build beautiful churches or temples, but to cultivate positive human qualities such as tolerance, generosity and love. Every world religion, no matter what its philosophical view, is founded first and foremost on the precept that we must reduce our selfishness and serve others. Practitioners of different faiths should realise that each religious tradition has immense intrinsic value, and the means for providing mental and spiritual health. One religion, like a single type of food, cannot satisfy everybody. According to their varying mental dispositions, some people benefit from one kind of teaching, others from another. Each faith has the ability to produce fine, warm-hearted people.

CHAPTER 32

The Good Heart: A Buddhist Perspective on the Teachings of Jesus

• •

My main concern is this: how can I help or serve the Christian practitioner? The last thing I wish to do is to plant seeds of doubt and scepticism in their minds. According to my own experience, all the world's major religious traditions provide a common language and message upon which we can build a genuine understanding.

In general, I am in favour of people continuing to follow the religion of their own culture and inheritance. Let us take the example of meditating on love and compassion in the Christian context. In an analytical aspect of that meditation, we would be thinking along specific lines, such as the following: to truly love God, one must demonstrate that love through the action of loving fellow beings in a genuine way, by loving one's neighbour. One might also reflect upon the life of Jesus Christ himself, how he conducted his life, how he worked for the benefit of other sentient beings, and how his actions illustrated a compassionate way of life. This type of thought process is the analytical aspect of meditation on compassion. One might meditate in a similar manner on patience and tolerance.

Now I will read from the Gospel.

You have heard that they were told, An eye for an eye, a tooth for a tooth. But what I tell you is this: Do not resist those who wrong you. If anyone slaps you on the right cheek, turn and offer him the other also. If anyone wants to sue you and take your shirt, let him have your cloak as well. If someone in authority presses you into service for one mile, go with him two. Give to anyone who asks, and do not turn your back on anyone who wants to borrow.

(Matthew 5:38-42)

The practice of tolerance and patience, which is being advocated in these passages, is extremely similar to the practice of tolerance and patience which is advocated by Buddhism in general. And this is particularly true in Mahayana Buddhism, in the context of the bodhisattva ideals, in which the individual who faces certain harm is encouraged to respond in a non-violent and compassionate way. In fact, one could almost say that these passages could be introduced into a Buddhist text, and they would not even be recognised as traditional Christian scriptures.

You have heard that they were told, 'Love your neighbour and hate your enemy.' But what I tell you is this: Love your enemies and pray for your persecutors: only so can you be children of your heavenly Father, who causes the sun to rise on good and bad alike, and sends rain on the innocent and the wicked. If you love only those who love you, what reward can you expect? Even the tax-collectors do as much as that. If you greet only your brothers, what is extraordinary about that? Even the heathens do as much. There must be no limit to your goodness, as your heavenly Father's goodness knows no bounds.

(Matthew 5:43-48)

This reminds me of a passage in a Mahayana Buddhist text known as the *Compendium of Practices,* in which Shantideva asks, "If you do not practice compassion towards your enemy, than towards whom can you practice it?" The implication is that even animals show love, compassion and a feeling of empathy toward their own loved ones. As we claim to be practitioners of spirituality and a spiritual path, we should be able to do better than animals.

These Gospel passages also remind me of reflections in another Mahayana text called *A Guide to the Bodhisattva's Way of Life,* in which Shantideva states that it is very important to develop the right attitude towards your enemy. If you can cultivate the right attitude, your enemies are your best spiritual teachers, because their presence provides you with the opportunity to enhance and develop your capacity for compassion and, through that, altruism. So, even for the practice of your own spiritual path, the presence of an enemy is crucial. The analogy drawn in the Gospel, as to how the sun makes no discrimination where it shines, is very significant. The sun shines for all and makes no discrimination. This is a wonderful metaphor for compassion. It gives the sense of its impartiality and all-embracing nature.

As I read these passages, I feel that the Gospel especially emphasises the practice of tolerance and feelings of impartiality toward all creatures. In my opinion, in order to develop one's capacity for tolerance towards all beings, and particularly towards an enemy, it is important as a precondition to have a feeling of equanimity and compassion.

There are specific techniques for developing this sense

of equanimity toward all sentient creatures. In Christian theology, there is the belief that all human beings are created in the image of God — we all share a common divine nature. I find this quite similar to the idea of Buddha-nature in Buddhism. On the basis of this belief that all human beings share the same divine nature, we have a very strong ground, a very powerful reason to believe that it is possible for each of us to develop a genuine sense of equanimity and compassion toward all beings.

Bibliography

● ● ● ● ● ● ● ● ● ● ● ● ● ● ● ● ●

1. The Dalai Lama. *Cultivating a Daily Meditation.* Library of Tibetan Works & Archives, 1993.

2. The Dalai Lama. *The Dalai Lama at Harvard.* Snow Lion Publications, 1988.

3. The Dalai Lama. *The World of Tibetan Buddhism.* Wisdom Publications, Boston, 1995.

4. The Dalai Lama. *Kindness, Clarity and Insight.* Snow Lion Publications, 1988.

5. The Dalai Lama. *Mind Science.* Wisdom Publications, 1991.

6. The Dalai Lama. *The Path to Enlightenment.* Snow Lion Publications, 1995.

7. The Dalai Lama. *The Meaning of Life from a Buddhist Perspective.* Wisdom Publications, 1992.

8. The Dalai Lama. *Opening the Mind and Generating a Good Heart.* Library of Tibetan Works & Archives, 1995.

9. The Dalai Lama. *Four Essential Buddhist Texts.* Library of Tibetan Works & Archives, 1993.

10. The Dalai Lama. *Speeches, Statements, Articles, Interviews.* 1987 to June, 1995. The Department of Information & International Relations, 1995.

11. A.A. Shiromany. *The Spirit of Tibet: Universal Heritage.* Allied Publishers Limited, 1995.

12. The Dalai Lama. *The Bodhgaya Interviews.* Snow Lion Publications, 1988.

13. The Dalai Lama. *The Good Heart: A Buddhist Perspective on the Teachings of Jesus.* Wisdom Publications, 1996.

14. The Dalai Lama. *An Introduction to Buddhism and Tantric Meditation.* Paljor Publications, 1996.

15. The Dalai Lama. *Commentary on the Thirty Seven Practices of a Bodhisattva.* Library of Tibetan Works and Archives.

Glossary

Abhidharma	Pure wisdom
Afflictive emotions	Emotions that cause suffering for beings addicted to them
Anitya	Impermanence
Arhat	An awakened being on the threshold of Buddhahood
Arya	Noble, superior
Aryasatya	Noble Truth
Atman	Self
Avidya	Ignorance
Bhava	Existence
Bodhichitta	Altruistic mind of enlightenment
Bodhisattva	An awakened being on the threshold of Buddhahood
Buddha	An enlightened being
Chakras	Energy centres,
Chitta	Mind
Chakra Samvara	Cycle of time
Clear light mind	The extremely subtle mind of every living being
Dharma	To hold on to the truth
Dharmakaya	Truth Body
Dharmachakra pravartana	Turning of the Wheel of Dharma
Deva	God or deity
Dhyana	Meditation
Dukha	Suffering
Dvesa	Dislike
Guhyasamaja	Secret tradition
Hinayana	Individual Vehicle
Hetu	Cause

Kalpa	An extremely long period of time
Karma	Act, deed
Karuna	Compassion
Kaya	Body
Klesha	Defilement
Mahayana	Universal Vehicle
Mahashunya	The great emptiness
Mara	The tempter; forces of ignorance that hinder progress on the path to enlightenment
Marga	Path
Moha	Delusion
Nairatmya	Selflessness
Nirmanakaya	Emanation body
Nirvana	Cessation; freedom from cyclic existence
Nitya	Permanent
Pandit	Scholar
Paramarthasatya	Ultimate truth
Paramita	Perfection
Paramitayana	Perfection Vehicle
Parinirvana	Ultimate salvation
Prajna	Wisdom
Pratimoksha	Individual Liberation
Pratitya	Meeting, relying and depending
Pratityasamutpada	Dependent arising
Pratyekabuddhayana	Solitary Realisers' Vehicle
Preta	Hungry ghost
Rupakaya	Form Body
Samadhi	Meditative state
Samatha	Tranquil or calm abiding
Sambhogkaya	Complete Enjoyment Body
Samkhya system	Ancient mystical system
Samsara	The wheel of cyclic existence

Samtana samutpada	Continuum/mental continuum arising
Samvritisatya	Conventional truth
Sangha	The Buddhist community, one of the Three Jewels of Refuge
Sattva	Meditative quality
Shila	Precepts
Skandha	Aggregate
Smriti	Mystical saying retained in memory
Sukha	Joy, happiness
Sukshma	Subtle
Shunya	Empty
Svabhava	Nature
Svabhavasiddha	Inherent existence
Sutra	Brief mystical statement
Tantra	Tool
Tantrayana	Tantric Vehicle
Tathagata	'Thus came, thus gone'; one of the names of the Buddha
Tripitaka	Three baskets
Triratna	Three Jewels
Trishna	Desire, longing, attachment
Upadana	Grasping
Vajrayana	Diamond Vehicle
Vajrapani	One who holds the mystical weapon
Vijnana	Consciousness
Vipashyana	Insight, clear perception
Yana	Vehicle

The Foundation for Universal Responsibility of H.H. the Dalai Lama

The Foundation for Universal Responsibility of His Holiness the Dalai Lama was established with the Nobel Peace Prize money as its initial corpus fund. It promotes universal responsibility in a manner that respects and encourages a diversity of beliefs and practices; promotes and devises strategies to transform this commitment into an instrument of social change for personal happiness.

The foundation brings together people of different faiths, persuasions, professions and nationalities. It does not promote an individual or idea; instead, it seeks to bring together insights and techniques that will further its goals. To the Dalai Lama, it represents a reaching out beyond his role as the pre-eminent Buddhist monk and transcends the political agenda of a free Tibet.

The headquarters of the foundation are located in Dharamsala, where the Dalai Lama resides; its executive offices are in New Delhi. The foundation seeks to extend its activities and initiatives to benefit people in all parts of the world. In time, it will establish a global network of like-minded institutions through affiliation; it therefore emphasises participation and cooperation and welcomes your involvement.

"I think the most important thing is to develop a feeling for others, a feeling of closeness and trying to share their suffering. I believe this is not a matter of any particular religion, ideology or philosophy, but an expression of humanness. While I believe religion does help to develop a sense of universal responsibility, it is not necessarily so. If we can develop this genuine feeling of closeness, and a true understanding of interdependence, many of our personal and social problems can be solved.

The foundation will implement projects to benefit people everywhere. It will foster a commitment to universal responsibility amongst peoples. It will address the growing conflicts in the name of religion, facilitating harmony and cooperation between faiths. It will work towards assisting non-violent methods, on improving communication between religion and science, on securing human rights and democratic freedoms, and on conserving and restoring our precious earth.

It is a foundation established to act from the heart of the Tibetan people, to do good and helpful things not for their own country or followers of their faith, but for all people throughout the world.

No matter what part of the world we come from, we are all basically the same human beings. We all seek happiness and try to avoid suffering. We have the same basic human needs and concerns. All of us human beings want freedom and the right to determine our own destiny as individuals and as people. That is human nature.

People inflict pain on others in the selfish pursuit of their happiness or satisfaction. Yet, true happiness comes from the sense of inner peace and contentment, which in turn must be achieved through the cultivation of altruism, of love and compassion, and elimination of ignorance, selfishness and greed.

The realisation that we are all basically the same human beings, who seek happiness and try to avoid suffering, is very helpful in developing a sense of brotherhood and sisterhood, a warm feeling of love and compassion for others."

H.H. the Dalai Lama

Other Officers (1997-1998)

Tenzin Geyche*
T.C. Tethong*

Brig. S. Tripathi, *Consultant*
Raji Ramanan, *Projects Director*
Kunjo Tashi, *Administrative Officer*
Charu Manchanda, *Secretary*
Mini Rajan, *Accountant*
Ranji Dua, *Lawyer*
Munish Sharma, *Lawyer*
Sarvesh Srivastava & Co., *Chartered Accountants*
Srikant Chakravarthy, *Auditor*

---

*Member, Executive Committee

The Tibetan Book of Healing

by Dr. Lobsang Rapgay

"Dr. Lobsang Rapgay is one of the foremost Tibetan doctors in the world today and is also a psychologist. The *Tibetan Book of Healing* contains many helpful practices, going into diet, herbs and meditation and providing a number of methods and techniques to follow for self-healing purposes. It contains a wealth of information that will make the book a constant companion for those really seeking to improve their state of well-being." Dr. David Frawley, author of *Ayurvedic Healing: A Comprehensive Guide.*

"Having been the religious secretary to H.H. Dalai Lama and a monk, perhaps the greatest potency in this book is the clear and well laid-out approach for developing a well-grounded spirituality and meditation practice that he (Dr. Rapgay) offers in accordance with body/mind types and which people of all traditions can heartily embrace..."

Bob Sachs, author of *Health for Life, Secrets of Tibetan Ayurveda*

Trade Paper   ISBN 0-910261-40-7   201 pp   pb $12.95

Available at bookstores and natural food stores nationwide or order your copy directly by sending $12.95 plus $2.50 shipping/handling ($.75 s/h for each additional copy ordered at the same time) to:

Lotus Press, PO Box 325, Twin Lakes, WI 53181 USA
toll free order line: 800 824 6396   office phone: 262 889 8561
office fax: 262 889 2461   email: lotuspress@lotuspress.com
web site: www.lotuspress.com

Lotus Press is the publisher of a wide range of books and software in the field of alternative health, including Ayurveda, Chinese medicine, herbology, aromatherapy, Reiki and energetic healing modalities. Request our free book catalog.